SHORT WAL

East Kent Pubs

Chris Wade

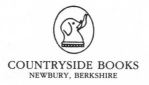

COUNTRYSIDE BOOKS
NEWBURY, BERKSHIRE

COUNTRYSIDE BOOKS
3 Catherine Road
Newbury, Berkshire

ISBN 1 85306 348 7

Designed by Mon Mohan
Cover illustration by Colin Doggett
Photographs by the author

Produced through MRM Associates Ltd., Reading
Typeset by Paragon Typesetters, Queensferry, Clwyd
Printed by Woolnough Bookbinding, Irthlingborough

Contents

Introduction

East Kent is such a diverse area, almost a county within itself. Mainland Europe has been knocking on the door for a long time and the reasons become obvious when you start your own exploration. The White Cliffs start to prop themselves up on one elbow and the North Downs kneel gently to the sea as the controversial tunnel runs beneath the English Channel to the not so far off shores of France.

History has had a busy time around Kent's eastern shoreline. It has the temerity on occasions to creep up behind you and blow gently down the back of your neck.

Every sense is stimulated by the unfolding countryside. There is not only the discovery of what part it may have played in the past, but also the constant surprise as changing seasons ensure that nothing, even areas you think you already know so well, can be taken for granted. Nature provides her creation with coats of various hues, textures and colour which seem to alter almost by the hour as the sun spreads light as though plotting points on a protractor. Man, too, has moulded the landscape to meet the demands of an ever-growing population, adding vivid splashes of green, yellow and sometimes blue to supplement nature's paintbox; at other times a broad brush of browns.

The walks in this book lead you through this landscape. Kent's countryside is definitely a working one. You may therefore find livestock sharing the fields with you. Your path may have been ploughed and not yet re-defined. The paths may well be muddy or wet. But I am sure that, with consideration and suitably shod, you will obtain great enjoyment from and respect for the East Kent countryside from its rights of way network.

The most useful OS map to further enhance your enjoyment of these walks is a 1:25 000 scale Pathfinder. With about 2½ inches to 1 mile they also show public rights of way in green and other helpful information such as field boundaries. I have included the relevant map number for each walk.

Each walk starts and finishes at a good pub where you will be well fed and watered. Permission has been given for cars to be parked at the respective inns while you undertake your walk, assuming that you are going to patronise the establishment either before or after, of course. My family and I have gained enormous pleasure from all of these walks and I sincerely hope that you find them equally as enjoyable.

Finally, I would like to thank my wife Carol and my sons Philip and

Stewart for their assistance. Thanks too to Gillian Whyte, for her sterling efforts.

The Country Code should be observed at all times and is as follows:

Enjoy the countryside and respect its life and work.

Guard against all risk of fire.

Fasten all gates.

Keep dogs under close control.

Keep to public paths across farmland.

Use gates and stiles to cross fences, hedges and walls.

Take your litter home.

Help to keep all water clean.

Protect wildlife, plants and trees.

Take special care on country roads.

Make no unnecessary noise.

Enjoy the hospitality of the chosen pubs and walk some of the footpaths and byways of this lovely county.

Chris Wade
Spring 1995

Publisher's Note

We hope that you obtain considerable enjoyment from this book; great care has been taken in its preparation. However, changes of landlord and actual closures are sadly not uncommon. Likewise, although at the time of publication all routes followed public rights of way or permitted paths, diversion orders can be made and permissions withdrawn.

We cannot of course be held responsible for such diversion orders and any inaccuracies in the text which result from these or any other changes to the routes nor any damage which might result from walkers trespassing on private property. However, we are anxious that all details covering the walks and the pubs are kept up to date and would therefore welcome information from readers which would be relevant to future editions.

Area map showing locations of the walks.

Wormshill
The Blacksmiths Arms

Sitting high on Kent's premier line of hills, the North Downs, the Blacksmiths Arms is located in Wormshill's linear village street. It is an old country inn with lots of character and among the features are exposed wooden beams in the bar and a cheery open fire to warm yourself beside on wintry days. The pub has a marvellous atmosphere and would, I am sure, meet most people's expectations of a typical country inn. Good value home-cooked meals are served. There are many specials, including steak and kidney pudding and rabbit pie, all with fresh vegetables. Bar snacks from sandwiches to soup are also available every day, except on Sunday evenings. There is a large garden to the rear for the warmer months but children and dogs are also welcome within the pub itself.

The Blacksmiths Arms is a freehouse, but beers available include Shepherd Neame Master Brew and Fuller's London Pride, and there is always one guest beer which is changed on a regular basis. You will find a large number of different lagers and ciders, should they be your preference.

The opening times are 12 noon to 3 pm and 6 pm to 11 pm during the week. The Sunday hours are 12 noon to 3 pm and 7 pm to 10.30 pm.

Telephone: 01622 884.

How to get there: Wormshill is to the south of Sittingbourne and north-east of Maidstone. Take the road that runs between Sittingbourne and Hollingbourne, the B2163, and follow the signposts off this road to Wormshill. The Blacksmiths Arms is on the southern outskirts of the village.

Parking: There is reasonable car parking adjacent to the pub itself. Careful and considerate parking is also available in the vicinity.

Length of the walk: 3 miles. Map: OS Pathfinder 1210 (inn GR 879571).

Wormshill is a sleepy village nestled in the north Downs. It is surrounded by a countryside of hidden valleys and woodland, interspersed with rolling pasture and arable fields. This walk is an exploration of a relatively unspoilt landscape that meets the expectations of our imagination. Despite its location on the North Downs the route involves only minimal amounts of climbing, making this an ideal walk for all ages.

The Walk

Having left the Blacksmiths Arms, turn left and, just after passing Yewtree farm, climb a stile in the hedge on your left-hand side and cross a large pasture field in a straight line, aiming to the right of a line of tall trees in front of you. These trees are in fact a small shaw and you pass by them, dropping into a small hollow and then climbing up into the top right-hand corner of the field, using a stone building as your sight line. Cross a stile and then another into a lane. Climb the two stiles opposite into a large arable field. Cross the field, using as an aiming point the junction at which the hedgeline in the distance to your left meets the hedgeline in the distance in front of you. Climb two stiles and either follow the track to your right for more refreshment at the Ringlestone public house or cross the pasture field in front of you and bear right towards the woodland in the distance, aiming just slightly left of the right-hand corner of the field. Enter the wood and follow the path through traditionally coppiced woodland. Unfortunately, coppicing has become uneconomical over recent years and the practice is now in some decline.

Leave the wood and cross the open field in front of you, aiming to meet the hedgerow coming in from your left-hand side at the point where it curves left again out of your sight. Shortly after passing under the high tension cables, climb a stile and continue in the same direction, with the fenceline on your right-hand side and typical rolling downland scenery opening up in front of you. The village of Wormshill is visible in the distance to your left. Skirt the ancient pond and climb two stiles before going diagonally left across a pasture field

9

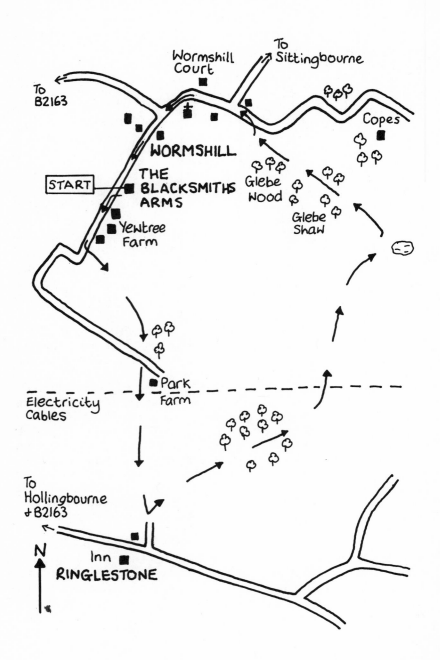

Sheep near Wormshill.

to enter a wood marked by a yellow-topped waymark post. The path goes downhill in a straight line and no sooner are you in the wood than you are out again, crossing a stile into a pasture field. The path goes diagonally right across the slope to the valley bottom, in line with the hedgerow that you see stretching up the hillside in front of you. Climb uphill (it's not too bad), keeping to the right of this hedgeline.

Go over the next stile into a small pasture field, crossing diagonally left towards the hedgeline which runs parallel to the road and using as an aiming point the right-hand side of the white timbered building in front of you. In the right-hand corner of this field cross a stile onto the road, which you now follow as it goes through the village of Wormshill, passing the church of St Giles. There are some delightful properties to admire as you walk through the village and in the winter months the smell of woodsmoke pervades the air.

Places of interest nearby
Passed near the end of this walk *St Giles' church* dates back in parts to the 13th century, although much of the present building is 15th century. Some fairly extensive restoration took place at the beginning of this century.

2 Doddington
The Chequers

The Chequers has sat in an imposing position in the village for over 500 years. In the days when stagecoaches ran between Maidstone and Whitstable it was an important posting place. The overhanging eaves outside and the oak beams supporting the two storeys inside give a good indication of its age. There was too, apparently, a large apartment in the roof where post boys and postilions slept while their passengers slumbered in the bedrooms below. Today's traveller is equally welcome at this extremely popular public house which is, we are assured, also host to four friendly ghosts.

The real ales are Shepherd Neame Master Brew, Spitfire and Bishops Finger, and draught Guinness is also available. The lagers include Steinbock and Hürlimann, with Dry Blackthorn and a variety of bottled ciders should you prefer. The vast majority of people opt for the local butcher's home-made sausages but other traditional bar food is available, including plaice, cod and scampi with chips, either in baskets or on plates, various salads, ploughman's lunches, pancake rolls and a vast array of sandwiches on either French or granary bread. You may like to try the locally made cheese. A vegetarian choice is always available. The menu is extremely flexible and can be adapted to individual requests, particularly in respect of child portions. Food is only served at lunchtimes but is available seven days a week. Children are welcome here and the upper bar has one small table with chairs set aside for their specific use. The large outer patio area is extremely popular in summer months.

The opening hours are 11 am to 3.45 pm and 7 pm to 11 pm on Monday to Thursday. On Friday and Saturday they are 11 am to 11 pm, with Sunday hours being 12 noon to 3 pm and 7 pm to 10.30 pm.

Telephone: There is no publicly available telephone number.

How to get there: From the Maidstone to Ashford road (A20) turn northwards at the village of Lenham, following the signs to Doddington across the Downs. From the A2 between Sittingbourne and Faversham, Doddington is well signposted. The Chequers sits at a major road junction and for that reason is very easy to find.

Parking: The Chequers has a large car park or there is ample parking on the main roads through the village.

Length of the walk: 2½ miles. Map: OS Pathfinder 1210 (inn GR 935573).

Doddington is an attractive village lying snugly in that part of the county known as the Newnham valley. It can be realistically described as a true part of rural Kent. The walk itself takes you on a journey through both arable and pasture fields, woodland and small copses, dropping in and out of sunken valleys. It also gives elevated views over the village of Doddington, and gently traverses a rolling countryside.

The Walk

Leave the Chequers and turn left to the T-junction. Turn right to follow the footway next to the road signposted 'Wichling' and 'Lenham'. When you reach the butcher's shop turn left and follow the narrow road uphill past the village hall. At the brow of the hill turn right to follow a field edge path, keeping the hedgeline to your right and enjoying the open views that may be glimpsed through gaps in the bushes down to the village below.

After approximately 100 yards you will reach a gap, marked with a post, in the hedgeline. Turn left at this point across the arable field, following a defined path to the woodland in the distance. Doddington Place is visible to your left. Aim to reach the woodland 50 yards in from its right-hand edge. Enter the trees next to a substantial oak and follow the track that meanders generally right through the chestnut

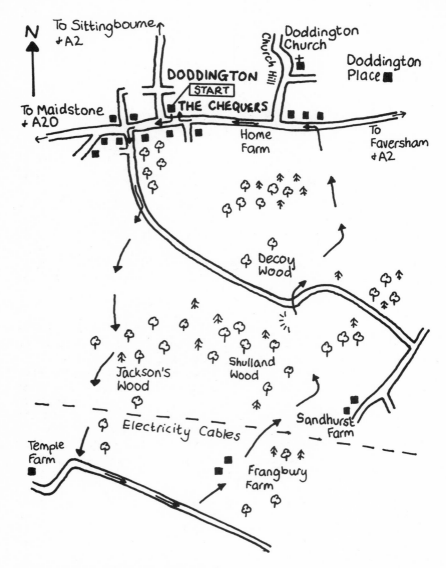

trees. Plastic yellow tape hangs from certain trees to guide you.

Enter an arable field and, keeping the woodland boundary to your left, continue to pass under the electricity cables in front of you. The path continues, running approximately 20 ft to the right of the woodland edge but this distance diminishes gradually as you progress

14

An old family butcher, at Doddington.

until eventually you meet the woodland edge at its junction with a road. Turn left to follow the road as it dips gently downhill and then back uphill again through open countryside.

Once the road levels out you will shortly see farm buildings to your left. Turn left to follow the broad track that takes you past these charming old buildings. Leave the track in front of the entrance to Frangbury Farmhouse and skirt the boundary fence, passing the properties to your left. At the end of the fenceline the path goes off to your right, crossing the arable field to the far right-hand edge of the strip of woodland in front of you. The path passes about 25 yards to the left of the electricity pylon to meet the woodland almost in the corner.

Enter the woodland and follow a waymarked path that meanders gently downhill to a stile. Cross the stile into a pasture field and continue heading for the left-hand edge of the boundary fence, which stands between you and buildings in the far distance. Shortly before reaching the fence turn left onto a defined track.

Follow this, passing the corner of the woodland to your right, and then leave the track to cross the pasture, heading for the hedgeline to your left. Aim to meet the hedgeline at a point approximately 50 yards from the opening into the road. (If you cannot see the road or even hear the occasional traffic, it is identified for you by the line of telegraph poles.) At this point you will find a stile. Cross this and continue, passing a small gully to your left before meeting the road. Turn right and then immediately left to follow a broad woodland track. Eventually the wood thins and you follow the hedgerow on your right as you progress across an open field. Here you will have a majestic view across the valley to Doddington church in the distance to your left and Doddington Place, as your eyes sweep back, in front of you and towards which we now appear to be walking.

When you reach a gateway in the hedgeline, turn left and head diagonally across the field, using the church as an aiming point. In the winter months the pheasants and partridges resident in the woods and fields through which you have traversed and no doubt startled by your presence will suddenly fly up and, in their turn, startle you.

Pass through the gap between two small trees and through a little hollow to continue across the field to join the road at the gateway clearly visible in front of you. Carefully cross the road and then simply turn left to follow the footway back to the Chequers, or digress if you wish to explore the church, which is close by, before returning.

Places of interest nearby

Doddington Place Gardens makes a pleasant outing after the walk. Here you can explore the Edwardian rock garden, a sunken garden, various flower gardens and woodland areas. Local crafts can be purchased in the visitors' centre. Telephone 01795 886385 for opening times.

Pluckley
The Dering Arms

Although the Dering Arms has been operating as an inn for 180 years
it was originally built as a hunting lodge and still retains its ostler's bell
today. The lodge was refurbished by the early Victorians and when
you investigate the interior the first thing you will note are the high
ceilings. There are, however, welcoming fires in each bar on cold days
and the resident ghost is an old lady who sits in the bar still dressed
in the clothes of the last century. People do wear old attire when out
rambling so if you are mistaken for the ghost do not be too offended.

The food here is superb with fish dishes being a speciality, fresh fish
being collected daily from Hythe. The menu board lists various steak
meals and a variety of pies served with fresh vegetables. Bar snacks,
including soup and ploughman's lunches, are served to suit the smaller
appetite. There are normally five speciality desserts. These change but
may include such delights as chocolate and chestnut slice with orange
and Cointreau and banana pancakes. A popular cheeseboard selection
includes Stilton and Cheddar. Smaller or half portions are available for
children, who are welcome in both the restaurant and the large
garden. Various beers are served, both bottled and draught, with
Goacher's of Maidstone brews a speciality. For the lager drinkers

Heineken and Stella are on offer. Local Biddenden cider supplements the more usual ciders.

The opening hours are from 11.30 am to 3 pm and 6 pm to 11 pm on Monday to Friday, with a half an hour earlier start on Saturday. On Sunday the hours are from 12 noon to 3 pm and 7 pm to 10.30 pm. Telephone: 01233 840371.

How to get there: Pluckley lies on minor roads west of Ashford. From the Tenterden direction and the A28 follow the signs through the village of Bethersden to Pluckley. The village is also signposted from Charing on the A20. From all directions follow the further signs to the railway station. The Dering Arms is just 100 yards away. Pluckley is on the Charing Cross line to Ashford and Folkestone via Tonbridge.

Parking: Outside the Dering Arms or the adjacent British Rail car park.

Length of the walk: 2½ miles. Map: OS Pathfinder 1230 (inn GR 922434).

Pluckley is said to be the most haunted village in Kent and plays host to a variety of ghosts. Listen out for the screaming man as you pass close to the Pluckley Brickworks. The village appeared in the ITV series 'The Darling Buds of May' and for both reasons attracts a number of visitors. It is a place of tremendous character. The route allows you to explore some of the exquisite countryside, walking through pasture fields and woodland. It is in no way strenuous although there are two tall ladder stiles to negotiate.

The Walk

Turn immediately left outside the Dering Arms to follow a broad track, passing to your left properties made from local stone. Go through the gate at the end of the drive and cross a small pasture, aiming for the left-hand edge of the woodland in front of you and following a well defined path. Climb the stile next to a large tree and go over a sleeper bridge. Turn right to skirt the edge of a huge arable field, following a track waymarked by yellow arrows with 'SETR' embossed upon them.

As you wend your way, no doubt you will see the railway to the right and will certainly hear the trains. When you approach the wood, however, all you will hear is the sound of woodland birds and the tinkling of the stream beside you. Stay on the clearly defined headland path beside the wood, which eventually runs parallel to the railway. Climb the ladder stile in the railway fence and cross the railway itself, taking extreme care. Climb another ladder stile to follow a well defined broad track through ancient woodland, with oak standards

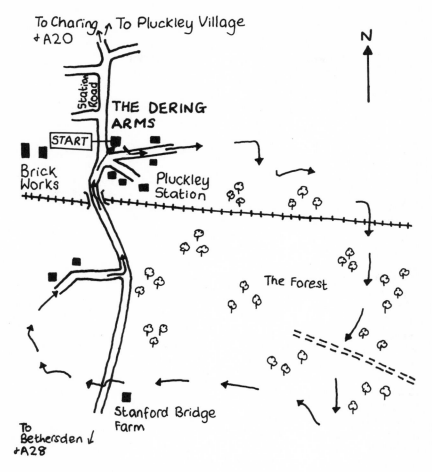

parading like sentries. Ignore any turning to your left and right. In spring and summer this area is carpeted with woodland flowers of all descriptions and in later months it is a riot of autumnal colour. Continue in the same direction when you meet a crossroads of woodland paths. The path narrows down before it reaches a T-junction. Turn right to follow a little path to the woodland edge.

Climb the stiles as you continue, keeping the woodland edge on your right-hand side and open pasture to your left. Go through a gateway into another, but larger, pasture field. In the distance you will see a group of farm buildings to your left. Cross the pasture field, aiming to pass to the right of these buildings towards the hedgeline in the distance. Just to the right of the field gate in this hedgeline you will eventually see a stile. Climb this into the road and turn left. Just before the large black barn, turn right to climb another stile into an open pasture field. As you stand in front of this stile you will see a large property with white painted windows. Aim across the field to the left-hand side of that property, also passing to the left-hand side of the lone tree in front of you. Beyond this tree, another and a yellow-topped marker post indicating the position of the stiles in the hedgeline, which you cross. Turn left to climb another stile by a small pond into a further pasture field.

Aim now for the telegraph pole to the left of the property in front of you. Climb two stiles and turn right to follow the road, passing some extremely interesting properties. When you reach the main road turn left. The house opposite has a sign 'Caution for Cats'. But please, the road is busy so caution for cars as well. Walk, facing the oncoming traffic, over the railway line to turn right to the Dering Arms and your car.

Places of interest nearby
The village of Pluckley is said to be one of the most haunted in Kent. Look out also for the strangely shaped casements, known as Dering windows after Lord Dering.

A feline warning outside a local house.

High Halden
The Chequers

4

The Chequers is a historic Kentish hall house dating back to the 14th century. It sits at the heart of the village, bedecked with virginia creeper, and looks towards the village green, church and former school buildings. The brick front of the house hides ancient timber beams, said to be from wrecks of old English galleons. As you would expect with a public house of such antiquity there are welcoming log fires in the bars during the colder months of the year. A very large garden to the rear extends the accommodation during warmer weather.

Food is served every day from noon to 2 pm and 7 pm to 9 pm, the evening hours being extended on Fridays and Saturdays to 9.30 pm. The Chequers provides traditional country foods such as home-made steak and kidney pie, liver and bacon and jacket potatoes, plus steaks and seafood dishes which include a selection from Dover sole, lemon sole, skate, haddock, mussels and king prawns. Children are catered for and portions adjusted accordingly. The whole range of Shepherd Neame beers are available including Spitfire and Master Brew. Among the lagers are Hürlimann, Beck's and Grolsch and the cider drinkers have Scrumpy Jack plus other bottled varieties. Opening hours are

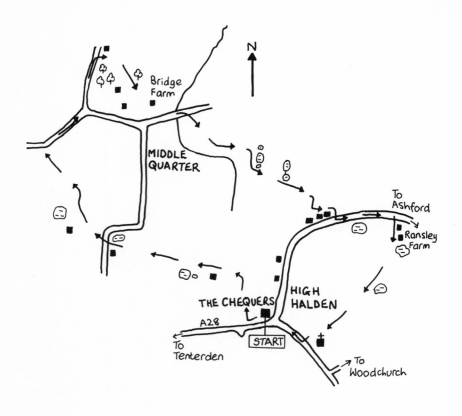

from 11 am to 3 pm and 6 pm to 11 pm on Monday to Thursday, 11 am to 11 pm on Friday and Saturday and 12 noon to 3 pm and 7 pm to 10.30 pm on Sunday. Bed and breakfast is also available.
Telephone: 01233 850218.

How to get there: Simply follow the A28 between Ashford and Tenterden. High Halden sits just to the north of Tenterden and the Chequers is at the heart of the village, overlooking the village green.

Parking: Car parking is available at the Chequers or around the small triangular village green opposite.

Length of the walk: 3 miles (short cut possible). Map: OS Pathfinder 1250 (inn GR 900373).

The route provides an ideal opportunity to witness a pastoral landscape, parts of which appear to have remained unchanged for centuries. The terrain is flat and provides easy walking and there seem to be ponds simply everywhere – we call this 'The Pond Walk'. The church of St Mary the Virgin is also worthy of your time, with its interesting wooden tower.

The Walk

From the Chequers turn right to Moriartis Workshop (pine furniture) and turn right to follow a footpath running beside a small Tudor-beamed building. Follow the surfaced path, passing a factory area to your right. Climb the stile into the cricket field. Pass to the right of the pavilion, crossing the field to a stile in the far hedge. Climb the stile and continue in the same direction to the gate in the boundary hedge, just to the right of the first of a number of ponds to be passed on this walk. Climb the stile beside the gate to enter a large arable field. Cross the field, aiming to pass to the right of the telegraph pole in the middle of the field and ultimately to the oak tree in the far right-hand corner. Climb the stile beside the oak tree and follow the boundary of the next field to another stile beside a pond and onto the road. Turn left and immediately right to cross a stile into a pasture field. Turn right and continue across the field, aiming to pass between the two telegraph poles towards the right-hand edge of the hedgeline you will see in the distance.

Go through the gate and proceed, keeping the boundary hedge to the next field on your right. Go through the next gate and straight across the field to the right-hand edge of the mature hedgerow, where you will climb a stile to meet the road opposite a pond. Turn right and proceed along a wide, grassed verge on the left of the road. After passing another pond on your right turn left at the road junction. Ignore the footpath signposted to your left but continue, passing Little Acorn Farm on your left and enclosed woodland to your right. At the far end of the wood turn right and, keeping the woodland boundary fence to your right, continue, eventually meeting a double-fenced path that leads you to a small field where you climb the stile into the road and turn left.

Cross the road bridge and turn immediately right over the stile into horse paddocks to follow the stream that runs to your right. Ignore the path that goes off to your right but continue into the corner of the field and cross a stile there. Having crossed the stream, turn left to follow a headland path. Some 25 yards from the corner of the field turn right and follow the path as it keeps to the right of three ponds. Having passed the third pond, turn left to climb a stile. Follow the headland path into the corner of the next field.

Ignoring the stile here on your left, cross the stile in front of you.

High Halden church.

Continue forward, keeping to the right of a line of oak trees. Cross the fence now, keeping a hedgeline on your left until you reach another stile. Having climbed this, follow the headland path as it winds its way around the field boundary to the road.

Here you may turn right and follow the footway back to High Halden if you wish.

To continue the walk turn left and proceed very carefully along this very busy road to the converted farm buildings. Climb the stile and proceed, following the boundary fence to your left. The fence is eventually replaced by a hedgeline which you continue to follow, ignoring all turnings to your left. Climb two stiles and follow the path across a pasture field towards the church in the near distance. Enter the churchyard through a wicket gate adjacent to a holly tree. Follow the church path as it goes off to the right and past the church to the road. Turn right to return to the Chequers.

Places of interest nearby
High Halden church has an extraordinary timbered porch – it has been standing here for 600 years. In the south porch two halves of an upturned tree form the arch.

Rolvenden
The Bull

(5)

The Bull is a noted hostelry of many years standing and in those far off days when punishments were administered locally the old lock up, known as the round house because of its shape, used to stand to the rear. The large room of the public house was converted on occasions into a police court. Today the pub retains its original charm and ambience. The original inglenook fireplace remains and the pub is unusual in so far as it has just the one bar, which has been erected dead centre, and service is given to the dining room from one side and the public bar from the other.

The menu is extensive and varied, with starters such as soup, melon, corn on the cob or pâté. From the main courses you may like to try the steak and ale pie, beef curry or one of the fresh fish dishes. Scampi is also available, and a number of steak meals. Bar snacks range from sandwiches and ploughman's lunches to jacket potatoes. All main meals are served with fresh seasonal vegetables. A three course 'Spoiler Night' is offered on Wednesday evenings. It is advisable to book for Sunday lunch. There are a variety of beers, including Webster's and several real ales of which Master Brew and Ruddles County are just two examples. The lager drinker has Foster's, Carling

Black Label and Kronenbourg. For the cider drinker draught Scrumpy Jack is available as well as others in bottles. You could sit in the large rear garden and watch the cricket in the summer months. Any children with you are welcome to use the variety of play equipment or go into the pub itself.

The Bull is open all day during the week from 11 am to 11 pm. The Sunday hours are 12 noon to 3 pm and 7 pm to 10.30 pm.

Telephone: 01580 241212.

How to get there: Rolvenden is to the south of Tenterden and as the A28 passes through the village turn right at the Motor Museum to find the Bull on your right.

Parking: There is a large car park adjacent to the Bull.

Length of the walk: 2½ miles. Map: OS Pathfinder 1250 (inn GR 844315).

Rolvenden stands on the summit of one of the many hills that give the Weald of Kent its undulating appearance. The walk gives an opportunity to sample a small slice of Wealden countryside as you head firstly towards Hole Park and then return to the village, passing the windmill and cricket ground on the way. The walk is flat and suitable for most age groups and levels of fitness.

The Walk

Leave the Bull and cross the car park towards the pottery shop. Turn right to follow a broad, double-hedged track, passing the pub garden to your right. Follow the track as it winds past the cricket ground, and above the hedge you will see the sails of the windmill in the distance. The sound of birdsong is all around you. Go between two marvellous ponds and through a gateway into a pasture field with wonderful open views across the countryside.

Aim to pass to the left-hand side of the hedge visible in the near distance to your right. Keeping the hedge to your left, drop gently downhill towards a Tudor-beamed cottage with oast houses to its right-hand side. At the base of the slope cross a stile and follow the broad track to your right, continuing downhill. After approximately 15 yards turn left onto a narrower path. Cross the footbridge and then climb the stile up the slope in front of you.

Continue to follow the woodland edge on your right. When the wood turns to the right continue across the field in front of you, going half-right to a gateway in the distant hedgeline. Do not go through the gate but turn left to follow the hedgeline. Go through a gateway into the farmyard and turn left to follow the concrete farm access road.

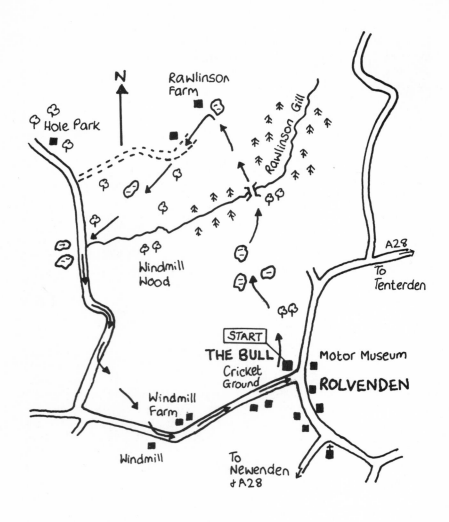

Pass the semi-detached houses to your right and cross the cattle grid. As the track curves to the right leave the road and follow to the left-hand side of three oak trees in front of you towards a field gate in the fence. Go through this gate and aim for the left-hand corner of the wooded pond that you can see to your right. Skirt the pond to its southernmost tip. Cross the field diagonally right to pass to the left-hand side of the oak trees in the corner of the field. Go through the gate opposite a pond and turn left onto the farm road.

Follow this road as it wends its way through marvellous parkland.

The Motor Museum, Rolvenden.

Shortly before reaching the main road you will pass animal stockades on your left. Just beyond climb the stile into the field. Cross the field, aiming to the left of the windmill. With the sheep grazing amongst the trees and the windmill in the distance providing a backdrop, this all combines to provide an idyllic countryside scene.

Go into the corner of the field and through a kissing gate onto the road. Pause to admire the wooden mill and then turn left and follow the footway, with Rolvenden church clearly evident across the fields to your right. Pass the half-timbered medieval house with stunning chimneys at Windmill Farm before, perhaps, stopping to browse in the pottery. Prior to returning to your car you may like to visit the Motor Museum in the street opposite.

Places of interest nearby
The *CM Booth Collection* of historic vehicles (at 63-7 High Street, Rolvenden) houses a particularly important array of Morgan cars along with other historic cars, motorcycles and bicycles. The attractively landscaped parkland and gardens around *Hole Park* are open to the public at certain times of the year.

6 Wittersham
The Ewe and Lamb

Wittersham, on the escarpment overlooking the Wallend Marsh, is synonymous with countryside and has an appeal which is easy to discern. The Ewe and Lamb has served the local community for a number of years now and it retains the characteristics of a typical village pub. It is very comfortably furnished, with low ceilings, exposed beams and an open fireplace in one corner. It is even more welcoming when the pub cat comes and personally greets you as you enter.

The pub serves bar meals, which may include a ploughman's lunch, ham, chicken or cheese sandwiches, jacket potatoes with various fillings and sausages or chicken and chips. This menu is normally enhanced by a daily special. There are a number of beers available, including Beamish Irish Stout, John Smith's, Courage Directors, and for the lager drinkers Kronenbourg and Foster's. Dry Blackthorn and other bottled ciders are also on offer as is freshly brewed ground coffee. Children are most welcome either inside or in the adjoining garden, but if you are visiting the pub after you have carried out your walk please remove any muddy boots.

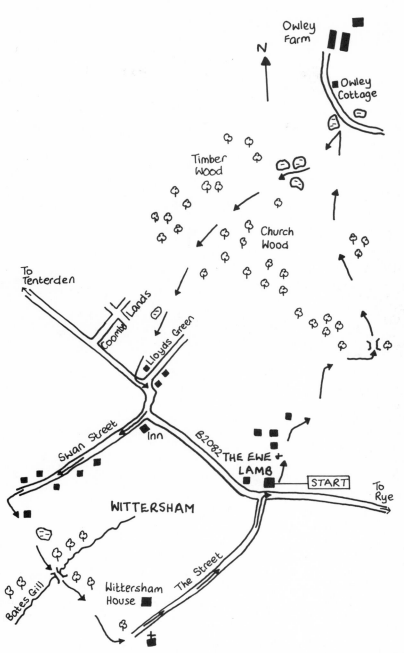

Owley Farm

N

Owley Cottage

Timber Wood

Church Wood

To Tenterden

Coombe Lands

Lloyds Green

Swan Street

Inn

B2082

THE EWE &
LAMB

START

To Rye

WITTERSHAM

The Street

Bates Gill

Wittersham House

Wittersham church.

The opening hours are from 11 am to 3 pm and 7 pm to 11 pm all week (10.30 pm on Sunday).
Telephone: 01797 270107.

How to get there: Follow the signposted road from the western end of Tenterden, the B2082, into Wittersham. The Ewe and Lamb will be found on the left opposite the war memorial.

Parking: There is restricted car parking at the Ewe and Lamb but ample room in the street opposite – please park considerately, though.

Length of the walk: 2½ miles. Map: OS Pathfinder 1271 (inn GR 901273).

This route combines the opportunity for a delightful exploration of the village of Wittersham and its church with a stroll through a working countryside and ancient woodland, discovering two remarkably hidden streams as you go. A marvellous walk suitable for all ages, although there are some rustic steps to negotiate.

The Walk

Take the surfaced path that runs along the left-hand boundary of the Ewe and Lamb. Skirt the housing development to the estate road. Go over this and walk across a small grassed area to cross a stile in the fenceline. Walk straight across the arable field to a yellow-topped marker post in the far hedgeline. Turn right and follow the boundary hedge until you reach a stile. Climb the stile and negotiate the slope down into a wooded linear valley. Cross the bridge over the stream before climbing up again to go over a stile into a large arable field. Continue in the same direction, aiming to pass under and to the right-hand side of the large oak tree that now appears to sit almost isolated in this huge field.

Having reached this oak, you will see two more beyond it. Pass to the right of these and proceed towards a white metal fence and field gate in front of you. At the gate turn, almost back on yourself, and follow a farm track diagonally left, heading out towards woodland just to the right of a telegraph pole. Pass between the ponds and turn left to follow an ancient hedgeline of chestnut and hornbeam as it leads you to the corner of the field. To your right there is a superb open countryside that appears to extend almost to Tenterden some miles distant.

In the corner of the field follow a narrow path into the woodland. Rustic steps take you down into an exquisite little valley (more of a gully, but to my children it was a valley) with a stream running through it. Cross the sleeper bridge over the stream and climb the steps in front of you – these may be slippery when wet. This little valley gives the appearance of a tranquil linear oasis in a desert of agricultural fields. It has an attractiveness at all times of the year.

Continue to follow the meandering woodland path. Cross the stile immediately in front of you into a small open field. Cross the next stile to follow a broad track. Pass to the right of a close boarded fence to walk between domestic gardens to the road, pausing as you do to admire the two ponds you encounter on the way. Cross the road, and go left to follow the footway until you turn right into Swan Street.

Continue down Swan Street. As you pass by you will see a number of wooden properties and a thatched cottage of tremendous character. Ignore the first two signposted footpaths to your left but at the third turn left onto a broad track. As you pass the white timbered cottage climb the stile into the next field. It may be that, as you walk along, the noises associated with the Kent and East Sussex Light Railway will drift across the fields, although the trains themselves do not appear to be visible from here.

Follow the fenceline to your left, passing to the right of the pond into the corner of the field to climb another stile. Follow the steps to stand on the bridge and pause for a while to marvel as the sunken stream beneath you continues to descend downhill on its journey through a narrow tree-lined gully. Continue to follow the double-fenced path, with orchards to your left and the graveyard to your right. Ignoring the stile on your left, continue in the same direction to join a broad, surfaced track, passing the orchards now to your right, until you reach the road opposite Wittersham's majestic parish church of St John the Baptist. Turn left and follow either footway through the village street, enjoying the variety of property lining the route. Some of it is old, some of it new, some large and others not so, but nearly all of extreme interest.

Eventually, after passing the war memorial to your right and the extremely unusual parish triangular garden of heathers, turn right and return to the Ewe and Lamb.

Places of interest nearby
At certain times of the year you can arrange to visit *Wittersham Mill.*

Conyer
The Ship Inn

7

Conyer Quay is a haven for the modern yachtsmen, but in the past was notorious for its association with the North Kent gang of smugglers who were 'mopped up' with the assistance of a Bow Street Runner by the name of James Bond. It is said the last smuggler returned to Conyer after years of exile and drowned in a storm. What is now the Ship Inn was originally built as a bakery for a nearby mill in 1642. As a pub it has been welcoming seafarers and other travellers for 200 years. The Smugglers Restaurant is decorated in maritime themes, including Davy Jones' Locker, The Dungeon, Sail Loft and Smugglers Contraband Store.

The varied menu includes seafood specialities and steaks plus a daily specials menu that may include lobster thermidor, Dover sole or dressed crab. Children's portions are available. You will find a wide range of bar snacks and desserts, from 'Paradise Island' to jam roly-poly. Vegetarians are also catered for. It is advisable to book a table in advance at weekends. In the bar five handpumps supply an ever-changing range of real ales which may include Aunty Doris's 90th Birthday Celebration Ale. Other beers available could be Adnams Ordinary, Ruddles County and Fuller's ESB. A sixth handpump

35

dispenses the local Biddenden cider. For the lager drinker Grolsch, Carlsberg, Foster's, Stella, Hürlimann are all on offer. The House speciality, however, is whisky – there are some 250 in stock, including more than 175 malts.

The Ship Inn is open daily from 11 am to 3 pm and 6 pm to 11 pm, with the restaurant staying open for an additional hour. On Sundays the hours are 12 noon to 3 pm and 7 pm to 10.30 pm.

Telephone: 01795 521404/520778.

How to get there: Halfway between the cities of Rochester and Canterbury on the A2 lies the village of Teynham. Conyer is signposted from here and the Ship Inn sits delightfully on the edge of the creek.

Parking: There is a small amount of car parking space adjacent to the Ship, otherwise park on the road in the village itself.

Length of the walk: 2 ¾ miles. Map: OS Pathfinder 1194 (inn GR 961648).

This is still one of Kent's loveliest shores and the walk enables us to explore the village and then turn inland to visit the wonderful fruit orchards of Teynham which, history tells us, may be the descendants of some of the first orchards planted on the orders of King Henry VIII's fruiterer, Richard Harrys.

The Walk

On leaving the Ship turn right and follow the road until it bends sharply to the left. At this point you will see a broad track going off to your right leading to the Swale Marina. Take this and almost immediately turn left onto another broad track and then immediately left again to follow a narrow path which wends towards the boundary of a housing development and eventually takes you into an orchard. Simply follow the boundary hedge, on your left, passing underneath the electricity cables and crossing a small bridge as you progress through the orchard.

The orchard is left behind as you enter an open field of blackcurrant bushes, now allowing open views across the village of Teynham, with the railway station clearly evident in front of you. Turn left and continue, keeping the boundary hedge on your left-hand side as you follow the field edge path, eventually passing a corrugated asbestos farm building. Ignore the tracks going left and right but continue in the same direction on a surfaced track which is bounded on both sides by orchards. Pass the Waste Water Treatment Works to enter a much narrower path running beside allotment gardens. Climb the metal stile

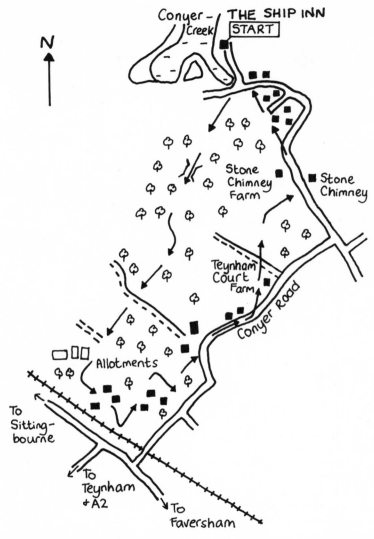

and follow the defined path between paddocks of grazing horses and donkeys. (You are asked not to feed the animals.)

Pass in front of the cottages (Station Row) and follow the roadway towards an old weathered brick building. Almost immediately before reaching the building turn left and follow a narrow path which turns right; once again you are sandwiched between paddocks of grazing

37

Conyer Creek.

horses. Eventually you will reach a farm access road where you turn left and head slightly uphill, passing through a farmyard to reach the road.

Turn left here (the road is narrow and traffic is not heavy but caution is still advisable). Proceed past a number of interesting properties on your left and at the point where you reach a row of terraced cottages on your right, turn left and climb a stile in the hedgerow to enter another orchard.

Cross the orchard diagonally left, walking between the trees, closely planted at this point, and crossing through two field boundaries of alder trees. To assist you with your navigation, aim to pass to the left of the telegraph pole almost immediately in front of you and then aim for the electricity pylon, which can be easily identified from the others in view by the fact it has no conductor terminals, the wires seeming to link with the frame of the pylon itself.

Cross a wide farm track, through a gap in another boundary of alder trees, to follow a broad, grassy track with fruit trees to your left and a defined boundary hedge to your right. In the corner turn left for approximately 25 yards then go right through a gap in the boundary trees to follow another broad, grassy track to the road, where you turn left.

Soon after passing the village sign for Conyer (Teynham),

underneath the high voltage electricity cables, climb the stile on your left-hand side and follow a double-fenced path, which eventually leads you to the road opposite the Brunswick Arms public house. Turn left and follow the road as it leads you back through the village of Conyer to the Ship.

8 Selling
The Rose and Crown

Selling is an extremely pretty village surrounded by orchards and hop fields and the area is enhanced by Perry Wood, one of the most attractive parcels of woodland anywhere in the county. The Rose and Crown sits like an oasis in an extensive landscape of trees. It is extremely popular with the many people who come to enjoy the pleasures of the surrounding woodland and, having visited this public house, become captivated by its friendly atmosphere. All the bars are very comfortably appointed and the two inglenook fireplaces add to the 'olde worlde' charm. The pub has a resident ghost, too. The back bar contains a number of bygone curios and some old photographs which depict the surrounding area as it once was. All in all a marvellous ambience. You may, of course, in warmer months, prefer to sit in the garden where children can enjoy the slide, swing and rocking horse in the play area.

The comprehensive menu is home-cooked and you may be tempted by a simple leek and potato soup or something more substantial such as a filled baguette, pheasant pie, vegetable stroganoff, chicken madras or chicken and mushroom pie. There are some excellent desserts but the favourite amongst those in the know is the chocolate roulade.

Children's portions are available, likewise vegetarian meals. There are a range of ales to suit all tastes, which include Shepherd Neame Master Brew, Flowers, Theakston and several guest ales. For the lager drinker Beck's, Stella and Heineken are normally available, but if your preference is cider then do try the Dry Blackthorn.

The opening hours are from 12 noon to 3 pm and 7 pm to 11 pm on Tuesday to Saturday (the Rose and Crown is not open on Mondays except for bank holidays). On Sunday the hours are 12 noon to 3 pm and 7 pm to 10.30 pm.

Telephone: 01227 752214.

How to get there: Leave the M2 (junction 7), the Thanet Way or the Boughton bypass at the Brenley roundabout. Follow the signposts across country to Selling. Just before entering the village turn left, signposted 'Perry Wood'. The Rose and Crown will be found after about ½ mile on your left.

Parking: Restricted car parking is available at the Rose and Crown. Parking is also available at the Perry Wood visitors car park nearby.

Length of the walk: 2 miles. Map: OS Pathfinder 1211 (inn GR 042552).

Perry Wood is an idyllic place for a ramble. It is carpeted with wild flowers in the spring and summer and in autumn a riot of colour, when children will love kicking up the leaves, as indeed will most adults, as they negotiate the paths. The elevated views are magnificent. There are some slight gradients as the wood covers a pair of hills. These pine and chestnut trees hide an ancient hill fort and a beech glade called the drawing room, a favoured picnic area. The walk could be easily extended if you wish.

The Walk

Leave the Rose and Crown and turn right to follow a broad track uphill, with open pasture to your left and woodland to your right. Digress to look at the Perry Wood information board. Continue on the broad track, turning right to skirt the large white house in front of you. Pass the house and turn right again. Ignore all tracks going off to your left and right but continue to follow the shingle-topped path through marvellous woodland.

As the path wends gently up and downhill and the trees start to thin out, look to your right to enjoy a superb landscape of orchards, hop gardens and oast houses that provides a typically Kentish backdrop of serene and tranquil countryside.

Ignore the shingle-topped path coming in from your left and continue in the same direction, ignoring too the next defined track

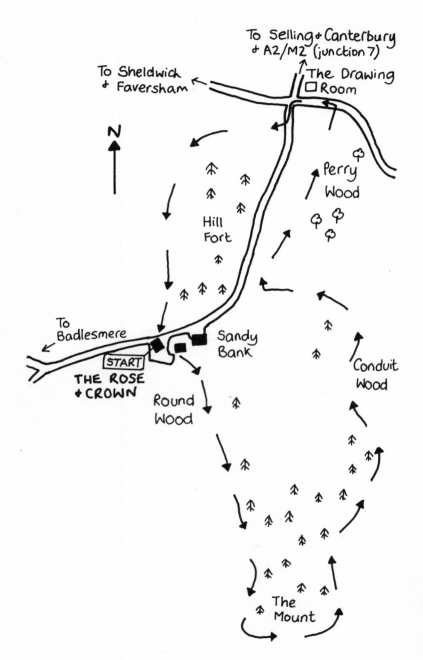

To Selling & Canterbury
& A2/M2 (junction 7)

The Drawing
Room

To Sheldwich
& Faversham

N

Perry
Wood

Hill
Fort

To
Badlesmere

Sandy
Bank

Conduit
Wood

START

THE ROSE
& CROWN

Round
Wood

The
Mount

going off to your right. Eventually, the route swings left as you pass close to the hop field on your right, again with marvellous views unfolding across the countryside for you. The path followed so far has taken you around a large mound which is sparsely covered with pine trees. Note how the woodpeckers have carved holes in some of the dead tree trunks and larger branches.

Continue to follow the broad track, ignoring all deviations. When you arrive at a track which leads to Keepers Cottage, cross this and drop down the incline in front of you. Go over a wooden causeway and turn right at the top of a short slope to continue through the chestnut woodland. Again stay on this main woodland track, ignoring turnings to your left or right. Go uphill through an area of majestic beech trees and silver birch and then downhill through rhododendrons to the road opposite Perry Wood visitors car park.

Turn left to follow the road, turning left again at the crossroads. After approximately 20 yards turn right through a gate into woodland. Follow uphill and bear right, ignoring the paths going through the pine trees in front of you. Bear right again to go around the right-hand edge of a large hollow with elevated views not only into the hollow but across open countryside to the sea in the far distance.

When you reach a small picnic area, take the track to your left which drops gradually downhill to reach the road opposite the Rose and Crown.

Hop garden near Perry Wood.

⑨ Boughton Lees
The Flying Horse

Boughton Lees has a superb village green at its heart, bounded on all sides by properties of varying ages; some very modern, some very old. The North Downs form a majestic backdrop. The Flying Horse is an old coaching inn standing on the Pilgrims' Way, overlooking the green. Exposed beams and inglenook fireplaces in the bars add to its character and charm. One of the results of recent sympathetic refurbishment was the discovery of two freshwater wells which the landlord has covered with glass so that customers may gaze down in addition to walking across. In summer months you can sit and watch the cricket from the front bar. To the rear there is a large garden and garden bar available in appropriate seasons. Children are welcome here and also in the separate dining room.

There is a full pub menu ranging from ploughman's lunches, sandwiches and sausages with chips to daily specials, which can include home-made steak and kidney pie, poached salmon and other fresh fish dishes. Puddings vary depending on the season or time of year. You will find an extensive range of beers and normally up to six different real ales, which may include London Pride, Old Speckled Hen, Wadworth 6X, Pedigree, John Smith's and Best. The lager drinker has Heineken and Stella, amongst others, to choose from and draught, dry and a range of bottled ciders are available for the cider drinker. You will be spoilt for choice.

The opening hours are 11 am to 3 pm and 6 pm to 11 pm (10.30 pm on Sunday). During the summer months the pub is open from 11 am to 11 pm on Saturday.

Telephone: 01233 620914.

How to get there: Boughton Lees lies just to the north of Ashford on the main A251, which leads to Faversham.

Parking: There is car parking available in the Flying Horse's car park. Otherwise, you can leave your car on the roads around the eastern and southern sides of the village green.

Length of the walk: 2½ miles. Map: OS Pathfinder 1231 (inn GR 022473).

In summer cricket is played on the village green and strategically placed benches allow you to tarry for a while before you continue on the walk through a marvellous and traditional English parkland to the remains of a ruined church beside a picturesque lake. The church is said to have royal association and is purported to be the burial place of Richard, last of the Plantagenets. Those who like an easy stroll will not be disappointed at any time of year.

Eastwell Park.

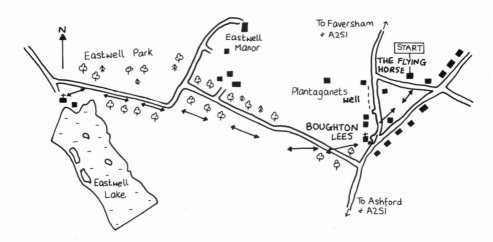

The Walk

From the Flying Horse proceed across the village green in front of you, skirting around the playing area of the cricket ground if there is a match going on in the summer. Pass either side of the war memorial towards the white building in the distance.

Cross the road carefully and follow the footway left and past St Christopher's church, a Baptist chapel. Shortly after go through a gate in the red-brick wall, signposted 'North Downs Way'. After negotiating the kissing gate proceed diagonally left across the field towards an avenue of trees and a gate in the fenceline. On your right you will see the historic roofs and chimney pots of Eastwell Manor in the distance. Go through the kissing gate and turn right to cross the road to negotiate another kissing gate into a further pasture field. Climb uphill diagonally right towards the fenceline, aiming for the clearly visible fingerpost. Having reached the top of the incline turn around and look back at the stunning backdrop of the North Downs, with the King Edward VII memorial crown carved out of the chalk.

Turn right and follow the level path, beneath a marvellous old tree, aiming for the water tower. Ignore the path waymarked to your right but continue in the same direction into the corner of the field. Pass through the kissing gate and follow a metalled road as it heads gently downhill towards the rolling countryside in front of you.

On your left-hand side you will see the splendours of Eastwell Lake, and further to your left the ornate towers marking the original entrance to Eastwell Manor.

Shortly after passing the entrance to the farm and Manor House, you will notice a metal gateway in a privet hedge. Turn left through this gateway and you will see the remains of Eastwell church in front of

46

you. Saint Mary's church, known as the 'Church by the Lake', suddenly collapsed in 1951 with a noise like a bomb. War damage and neglect had been the cause of its 'downfall'. The church had been built in the 14th century and contains the tomb of George James the 10th Earl of Winchelsea and the 6th Earl of Nottingham, born 31 May 1815 and died 9 June 1887. More romantically, however, it is said to be the site of the tomb of Richard the last of the Plantagenets, who died in 1550. With the inside wall of the tower in front of you the tomb will be behind you to your right. A stone erected on the grave states 'reputed to be the tomb of Richard Plantagenet'.

Having explored the church and soaked up the special ambience which seems to prevail here, simply retrace your steps over the route you have just followed, back to the Flying Horse at Boughton Lees. On the return journey the North Downs will frame the landscape for you. As you recross the drive to Eastwell Manor you will see a small memorial garden to your left. This is dedicated to the memory of two female employees who were tragically killed here.

Brook
The Honest Miller

Sheltered by the slopes of the North Downs, yet some little distance from their base, stands one of those superb small villages that are so frequently found in Kent. One of the best views to be obtained of Brook can be seen when driving from the direction of the A20. As you start to descend the hill you should stop and admire the village beneath you and the countryside to the right, of open fields and sheltered woodland through which the walk is soon to take you. The Honest Miller may give the appearance of an old, partially weatherboarded farmhouse. It does so for good reason for that indeed is what it once was. That transformation took place in 1871. The pub has gone through further more recent modernisation and one of its most innovative features today is the grill or sizzle stones which allow you to cook certain foods at your own table.

The menu is extensive and, as well as offering cook it yourself items, a choice ranging from sandwiches, steak and kidney pie, curries and chillies, lasagne and various fish dishes to steaks is normally available. Vegetarian meals are on offer, too. Banoffi pie is just one of the mouth-watering desserts. Children are welcome in the public house itself and will also enjoy the play area in the garden. There is a children's menu.

An extensive range of beers and real ales are served. You may like to try the Fremlins, Wadworth 6X, Winter Royal or Butcombe Bitter – or Stella, Heineken and Heineken Export for those who prefer lager. Bottled ciders and Scrumpy Jack are on draught for those who wish other options, as well as draught and bottled Guinness and Murphy's Irish Stout.

The opening hours on Monday to Saturday are from 11 am to 3 pm and 6 pm to 11 pm. The Sunday hours are from 12 noon to 3 pm and 7 pm to 10.30 pm.

Telephone: 01233 812303.

How to get there: Brook is signposted to the north from the A20 between Ashford and Folkestone. Follow the signs and proceed through the village street. The Honest Miller is on your right just below the North Downs.

Parking: You may leave your car in the pub car park.

Length of the walk: 3 miles. Map: OS Pathfinder 1231 (inn GR 069446).

This interesting route gives views of the Devil's Kneading Trough on the North Downs and takes you through woodland as well as pasture and arable fields. It is very easy walking and there are no hills to negotiate although you will find a number of stiles which need to be climbed.

The Walk

Leave the Honest Miller and go right on the main road to turn almost immediately right again, crossing a stile to follow the boundary fence. Marvellous views open up to your left across the ageless line of the North Downs with the Devil's Kneading Trough clearly evident, the striations caused by glacial activity thousands of years ago.

Cross another stile and, skirting the pond, follow the boundary fence on your left. Cross the stile in this fenceline and turn right. Cross the stream and continue in the same direction. At the edge of the woodland go straight across the field in front of you, aiming towards the stile beside a gate in the far hedgerow. Climb this and head over the rise towards the edge of the woodland visible before you. Soon you will see a stile; climb this into another pasture field. In the far distance you will see a house with a paddock to the rear. Walk across the pasture, aiming to the right-hand side of the paddock fencing.

As you proceed across the field you will notice on your right-hand side an old building surrounded by a moat, a very unusual feature in this landscape. Turn right at the far side of the moated area and head towards two gateways. Go through the left-hand gateway and

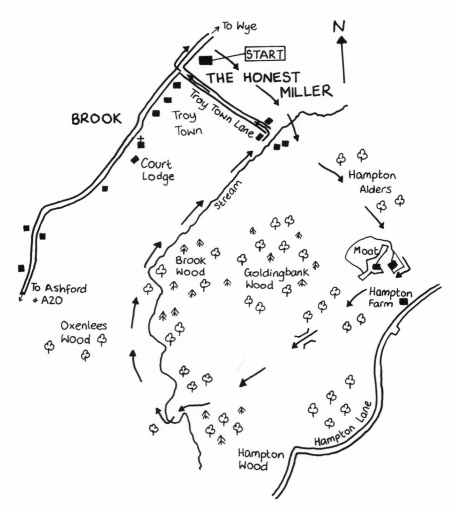

continue to follow the boundary fence on your right-hand side. You will be following an ancient hedgeline which leads you into the corner of the field, where you will cross the babbling stream, over a stile into a large arable field. Continue in the same direction across the field and as you broach the rise you will see a wide gap in the woodland in front of you. Aim to follow the track through this gap and across the next field to a tall single oak tree, where you turn right. Head towards the crown carved out of the chalk on the Downs in front of you, commemorating the coronation of King Edward VII.

The Devil's Kneading Trough.

At the point where the edge of the wood to your right meets the hedged boundary in front of you, you will find a stile which you climb to follow another woodland boundary. This is replaced, eventually, by a hedgeline and a fast running stream, which you continue to walk beside.

Cross the stile in the next hedgeline, turning left briefly before turning right to continue beside the hedgerow. Climb another stile and continue towards the white fronted building in front of you. Aim to pass to the right of this property, crossing the front lawn.

Climb the stile and turn left into Troy Town Lane, with delightful old buildings to admire before proceeding along the high hedged lane. A cornucopia of colour during the autumn and bedecked with wild flowers during other seasons. Turn right at the road to follow the footway back to the Honest Miller.

11 Ruckinge
The Blue Anchor

When you approach the Blue Anchor at Ruckinge from the east the first thing you will notice are two old redundant anchors in the car park. It is, however, hard to imagine today that at one time this pub used to stand on the beach. If you decide to sit in the back bar or the big garden then you will be able to look across Romney Marsh and the countryside from which the sea receded many centuries ago. The inn once had associations with the notorious smugglers of this area. In 1799 a cousin of the smugglers' leader George Ransley assaulted the landlord's wife. These days it is extremely welcoming with a reputation for value for money, home-cooked food.

The huge chalked menu board offers a multitude of choice from mussels, cauliflower cheese, stuffed mushrooms, home-made steak and kidney pie, grilled pork chops, gammon or steak to curries with poppadums and chutneys. Whatever you choose your portions will be generous. To slake your thirst there are five real ales, which are changed periodically. You might find Old Speckled Hen, Marston's Pedigree, Wadworth 6X, Brakspear and Fremlins. Draught and bottled beers include both English and Newcastle ales. Lager drinkers have a choice which normally includes Heineken, Heineken Export,

Budweiser and Beck's with Stella Artois on draught. Children are welcome, but not dogs.

The Blue Anchor is open from 11 am to 3 pm and 6 pm to 11 pm seven days a week. Food is served from 12 noon to 2 pm and 7 pm to 10 pm.

Telephone: 01233 732387.

How to get there: Simply follow the road, the B2067, that hugs the escarpment above Romney Marsh between Ham Street and Lympne. Ruckinge is just to the east of Ham Street and the Blue Anchor sits on the main road.

Parking: There is a large car park at the Blue Anchor.

Length of the walk: 3 miles. Map: OS Pathfinder 1251 (inn GR 026337).

The walk is extremely easy and follows a flat terrain through a landscape of pasture fields and woodland, allowing a glimpse of a marvellous piece of typical Kentish countryside.

Ruckinge church.

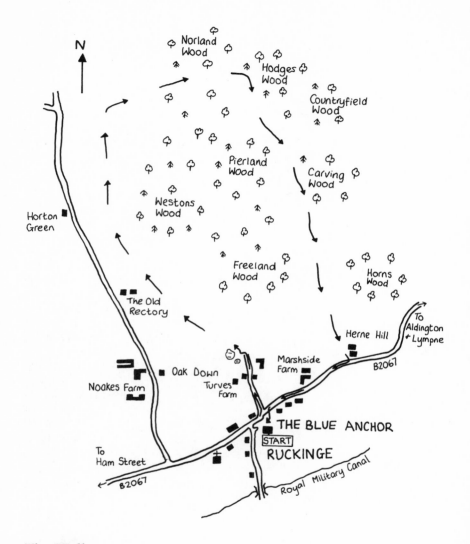

The Walk

From the Blue Anchor turn right into the road. Almost immediately turn left to follow a track signposted 'Turves Farm'. At the entrance to the farmhouse turn right and follow the track through the farm buildings into an open field. Follow the fenceline to your left and continue to follow the field edge to climb a stile to the right-hand side of a gate. Continue through the next field, with the woodland to your left. Ignore any gates or stiles that appear to invite you across the boundary to the left. As you reach the corner of the field cross another stile into woodland. Follow a marvellous sunken path bordered by ancient hornbeam trees to your right. Just before leaving the wood you pass an incredibly attractive pond on the right nestling in a natural hollow. Climb a stile and continue along an undulating sunken, grassy track with a fenceline high on the bank to your left.

Eventually, you follow a hedgeline and pass through a gate into a network of petite pasture fields divided by ancient hedgelines, interspersed with mature trees, that run off in straight lines to your right.

Pass these hedgelines and ignore the sleeper bridge and a stile in the hedgeline to your left and continue to the corner of the field. Climb the stile and turn right to follow a black-surfaced old lane which winds its way through the woodland, passing ancient oaks and offering views across more traditional pasture fields to your right and modern arable fields to your left.

Ignore any side tracks and continue through the woodland for almost ¾ mile. Even when the black shingle is replaced by a natural surface continue in the same direction. As the path descends to the road look across the fields to your right to Ruckinge church tower in the distance. Follow the concrete track past the weatherboarded house to the road. Turn right to follow the road, facing oncoming traffic, as it leads you back to the Blue Anchor.

If you still have the energy, continue past the Blue Anchor to the church. It is really well worth the digression. Look inside, of course, but also go around the church to the right and at the rear you will find a very rare graveboard which, legend has it, marks the burial place of George Ransley, the leader of the Aldington gang of smugglers. It is a Ransley grave, of that there is no doubt, but it is thought unlikely to be that of George Ransley himself.

⑫ Aldington
The Walnut Tree Inn

The Walnut Tree Inn is at the top of a fairly steep hill opposite the village green, where it has stood for several centuries. It was once the headquarters of the infamous Aldington gang of smugglers led by George Ransley, and the old well at the rear is said to be haunted by one of the smugglers who was murdered during an argument. Not knowing what to do with the body the other smugglers simply took what appeared to be the easiest option and deposited it in the well. Although it may have had a bloodthirsty past, as you enter the Walnut Tree you will note the welcoming and friendly atmosphere in both bars and restaurant today. No doubt you will notice, too, how the original decor gives a feeling of age. There is also a pleasant garden for the warmer months.

Shepherd Neame ales, including Spitfire, Master Brew and Bishops Finger are on offer. Hürlimann lager is on draught and you will find a full range of ciders. Food is served every day and is all home-cooked with a choice of starters or light meals, which might include ham, double egg and chips, jacket potatoes, welsh rarebit, and various sandwiches. A large selection of main courses include locally caught fish and game, venison and partridge being very popular main ingredients. Vegetarian meals are available. A traditional two course Sunday lunch is also served. Children are most welcome and child portions are offered. Dogs are welcome, but not in the main eating area.

The times of opening are on Monday to Saturday from 11 am to 3 pm and 6.30 pm to 11 pm, and on Sunday from 12 noon to 3 pm and 7 pm to 10.30 pm.

Telephone: 01233 720298.

How to get there: Aldington is found by leaving the A20 as it runs between Ashford and Folkestone and taking the B2069 southwards, which will lead you to the Walnut Tree Inn.

Parking: There is a spacious car park at the Walnut Tree Inn or you could leave your car in the layby opposite.

Length of the walk: 3 miles. Map: OS Pathfinder 1251 (inn GR 063366).

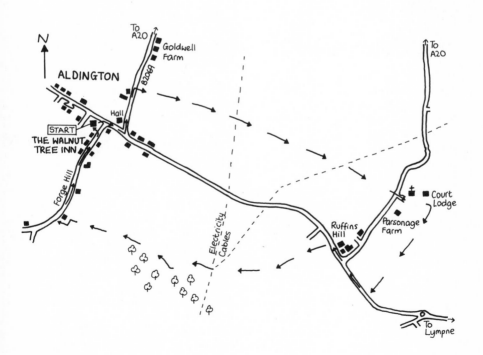

Duck pond at Aldington.

Aldington, on the ridge above Romney Marsh, has had long association with the smuggling trade and many of its public paths have wonderful local names reflecting that nefarious association, Cut Throat Alley and Smugglers Way to name but two. The walk is undulating and passes through an almost unique landscape offering stunning views across the Marsh itself, and it is not hard to imagine the 'gentlemen' smuggling their contraband across the paths and trackways of this still fairly remote area.

The Walk

From the Walnut Tree Inn, cross the road towards the village hall and turn left into Goldwell Lane. Shortly after passing Goldwell Close on your left, climb a stile next to a gate in the hedgerow on the opposite side of the road and, keeping the boundary fence on your left-hand side, follow the field edge towards the church tower visible in the distance. Go into the corner of the field and follow a narrow, defined path into the next large field.

Still using the church tower as your aiming point, cross this field on a broad, grassy track. As you do so you are rewarded, on your left, with superb views across open fields to the line of the ageless Downs in the far distance.

Enter a small farmyard with a solitary building and proceed straight across, through large farm gates to the road. Keeping in the same direction, follow a narrow lane to the church. Enter the churchyard and follow the path to the right of the delightful church with sheep grazing amongst the headstones. Go through the gate in the wall and turn right to climb the stile in the boundary fence. As you go over the stile you will enter a large arable field and in the far distance you will see a group of trees to the left of a 'power pole'. Aim to pass to the left-hand side of the trees which, as you get nearer, become more readily identifiable as a hedgeline.

When you reach the road turn right. Shortly after passing Church Lane on your right, pause to admire (from the road) the marvellous old barns at Ruffins Hill Farm, before continuing in the same direction for just over 30 yards to a signposted gate on your left, which leads you into a field where you follow the track at the base of the high embankment on your left. Aim for the gateway just to the right of the old sheep pens visible slightly to the right of centre in front of you. Go through this gate and aim to pass between the two electricity pylons, as you proceed diagonally downhill across the field towards a hedgerow. When you reach the hedgerow cross a sleeper bridge, climb the stile and turn left to follow a headland path beside the stream. In the corner turn right and continue, keeping the boundary fence on your left-hand side as you head towards a row of tall poplar trees, noting as you do the strange cliff line to your right-hand side, topped with a fence and what appears from this distance to be a stile.

Having reached the poplars climb the stile and continue in the same direction, with a fence on your right-hand side. Climb the next stile, cross the stream and continue uphill, with arable fields stretching off to your left as far as the eye can see. Also plainly visible are the electricity pylons, stomping with seven league boots across the countryside to the Dungeness nuclear power station.

Follow the field boundary as it meanders to the road where you climb the stile to turn right and follow the footway back uphill to the village of Aldington.

⑬ Dungeness
The Britannia

The vast majority of properties in this unique area are, almost without exception, single storey and are dwarfed by the two lighthouses and the power station. The Britannia fits in with this scheme and sits on the shingle, flanked almost equidistantly by the old and the new lighthouses. It is an ideal venue for families, close to the sea with the old lighthouse to be visited and the miniature Romney, Hythe and Dymchurch locomotives steaming into the nearby station. The building started life as two military block houses that were joined together following the end of World War II. The original public house was destroyed by fire shortly after but the modern version has risen from the ashes to become an extremely popular venue for sea anglers and others who, like me, are totally fascinated by this whole area.

The Britannia is gaining an excellent reputation for the standard of the home-cooked meals and its extensive menu. As you might expect, it offers locally caught cod and plaice purchased daily from local fishermen, and there are also plenty of choices not only for vegetarians but those who prefer something other than fish. Home-made steak and kidney pudding, various chicken dishes, lasagne and chilli con carne are but a few of the possibilities. The children's menu includes dinosaurs and chips. This is a freehouse and the real ales change regularly but there are normally four on offer. You may be able to sample John Smith's, Old Speckled Hen, London Pride or the strangely named 80/-. Foster's and Kronenbourg lagers are available in addition to draught Strongbow, Scrumpy Jack and other bottled ciders.

The opening hours are between 11 am and 11 pm on weekdays and from 12 noon to 3 pm and 7 pm to 10.30 pm on Sundays. These hours may be extended during the summer months.

Telephone: 01797 321959.

How to get there: Dungeness is at the southernmost point of the county. If approaching from Lydd turn right just before reaching the Pilot public house. If approaching from Greatstone turn left just after the Pilot. Follow the private road towards the lighthouse. The Britannia stands between the new and old lighthouses.

Parking: There is a large car park at the pub itself or you can leave your car on the compacted shingle nearby.

Length of the walk: 2¼ miles. Map: OS Pathfinder 1272 (inn GR 092169).

Dungeness sits on the largest area of shingle in Europe – and it continues to grow. The place is unique in almost every sense. It seems to have its own climate and it is renowned by anglers, bird watchers and photographers (who love the light) and those who simply enjoy its eccentricity. As the North Downs is a landscape of land, Dungeness, because of its flatness, is a landscape of sky. The walk for that reason is exceptionally easy going without one hill to climb or stile to negotiate.

The Walk

From the Britannia, turn right and, passing the terminus of the Romney, Hythe and Dymchurch Light Railway, head towards the power station and the old lighthouse. Just past the entrance to the lighthouse, leave the road to cross the shingle, following a narrow path towards the left-hand end of the black-roofed buildings surrounded by a grassy embankment visible in the near distance. In doing so you will pass two further domestic properties before reaching the surfaced road which leads to the black-roofed buildings. Follow this road until you can turn left to follow a path which runs around the base of the grassed embankment.

Eventually you reach a gap in the embankment on your right through which is a track to the cottages. Turn left at this point to follow a broad track and then bear right towards a line of old fence

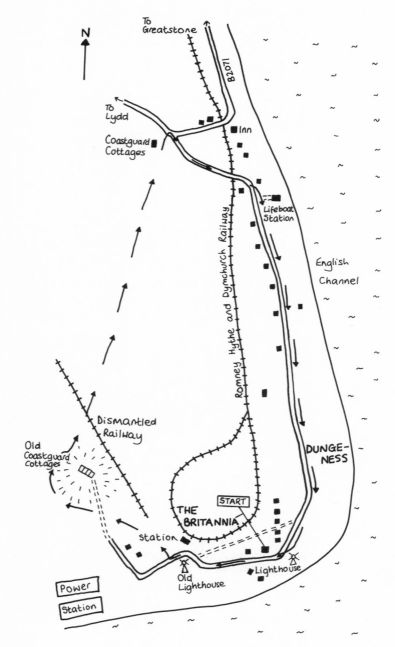

N

To Greatstone

B2071

To Lydd

Coastguard Cottages

Inn

Lifeboat Station

Romney Hythe and Dymchurch Railway

English Channel

Dismantled Railway

Old Coastguard Cottages

DUNGE-NESS

START

THE BRITANNIA

station

Power Station

Old Lighthouse

Lighthouse

posts in the distance. Pass between this old fenceline and continue to follow a clearly defined track, crossing an old railway line towards an area of stunted trees and bushes. Stay on the clear track, keeping your eyes and ears alert to the bird life here. At certain times of the year this is a haven for some of our migrant birds. You will almost certainly hear, in addition, the announcements ringing out from the power station behind you.

Very soon the vegetation is replaced by an open expanse of shingle, but the track still remains visible as it heads towards the right-hand side of the multi-chimneyed building in the near distance. Turn right to follow the surfaced drive as you reach this property and continue on it to the road where you turn right. Stay on this road now as it crosses the railway line and then bends right, running parallel to the sea.

At this point you will see a brick structure painted black. This is a tanning copper. These were used for dyeing and preserving fishing nets and aprons. The big circular copper tubs were filled with water and a fire lit underneath. Kutch (a resin from Burma) was placed in a basket in the water and slowly dissolved. When the water was a dark brown it was ready to receive the nets and clothing, which were soaked to preserve them against the ravages of seawater.

Continue to follow the left-hand side of the road as it passes the

Tanning tub at Dungeness.

lifeboat station, which is open to the public on occasions (admission free). Telephone 01797 367193 for further information.

The road leads you through a memorable landscape of shingle and domestic dwellings that have evolved and enlarged over the years, the like of which are not seen in such numbers anywhere else in the county. Prospect Cottage, for example, has a highly original garden of stones interspersed with flowers and metal sculptures.

Eventually you pass beneath the modern lighthouse and the track bends around to the right towards the old lighthouse again and the Britannia.

Places of interest nearby

The *Romney, Hythe and Dymchurch Railway* claims to be the world's only main line system in miniature! It is open daily from April to October. Telephone 01679 62353/63256 for times and fare details. The *Old Lighthouse* offers some outstanding views of the coast but there are 167 steps to climb first! Telephone 01797 321300 for further details.

14 Chartham
The Artichoke

The village of Chartham has been famous for its association with papermaking, which continues even today. The Artichoke is one of the 'historic buildings of Kent' and has the plaque to prove it. Parts of the inn date back to the late 1330s. It was originally a hall house and was once owned by Richard Marsh who founded the Shepherd Neame brewery. In 1675 he transformed the Artichoke into one of the first of what were known as brew houses, before moving on to bigger things with his brewery in Faversham in 1698. The interior of the inn reflects its historic past, with two inglenook fireplaces and original medieval windows. One very interesting feature in the restaurant area is the old well, cleverly converted into an eight-seater table with a circular glass top which enables diners to look through to the water below.

The reputation for excellent food has spread far and wide. There are bar snacks, which include a variety of sandwiches, ploughman's lunches and sausage, egg and chips, as well as à la carte meals ranging from home-made lasagne to a fillet steak with all the trimmings. Vegetarians are also catered for. Desserts include chocolate fudge gateau, strawberry gateau, profiteroles or banana split. There is a

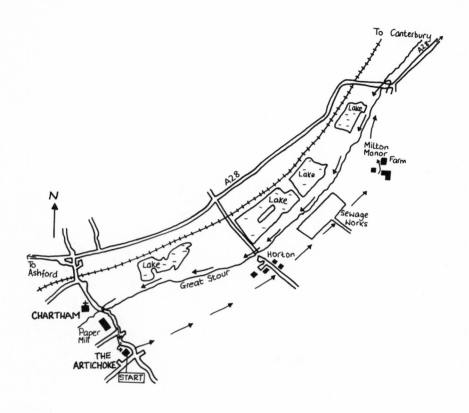

traditional Sunday roast and on the first Thursday of every month a set lunch for senior citizens. There is also a daily specials board. The whole range of Shepherd Neame beers are available, including Master Brew, Bishops Finger and Best Bitter. The lagers are Hürlimann and Steinbock and there is Blackthorn cider for those who prefer the taste of fermented apples.

The opening hours are from 11 am to 3 pm and 6.30 pm to 11 pm between Monday and Saturday and from 12 noon to 3 pm and 7 pm to 10.30 pm on Sunday.

Telephone: 01227 738316.

How to get there: Follow the Ashford to Canterbury road (A28). Chartham is well signposted. Go through the village, passing the paper mill. The Artichoke will be found just beyond, on the right of the narrow road as it starts to leave the village again.

Parking: Restricted car parking is available at the Artichoke. Off street parking is also possible in the near vicinity.

Length of the walk: 2½ miles. Map: OS Pathfinder 1211 (inn GR 109548).

The Great Stour flows through Chartham towards Canterbury and the walk enables us to explore not only the village but the tranquillity and charm of a small stretch of this river. The walking is totally flat, with just a few stiles to climb.

The Walk

Turn right outside the Artichoke to follow a narrow road bounded both sides by various properties of varying antiquity. Pass the old bakery, dated 13 June 1733, and then take a signposted footpath to your left. Go through the metal farm gate to follow a concrete track. As this bends to the left continue straight on across an arable field towards the hills in the distance. Aim to pass to the right-hand side of the red-roofed buildings. Cross the stile and follow a broad, surfaced lane. Paddocks with horses border the lane and on the left-hand side a group of derelict buildings, one giving the appearance of being an old church although from the visible timbers in the roof it was probably just a barn.

When you meet another track climb the stile in front of you and cross to the left-hand boundary fence. Continue in the same direction across paddocks with a variety of livestock, cows, calves and horses, grazing together. It is imperative that any dogs with you are under total control.

Pass the sewage works and climb a stile. The south facing slopes to your left seem to have regimented lines of fruit trees cascading down them. Climb the next stile to follow a broad, black-surfaced access road. Ignore the footpath to your left but continue in the same direction, passing the church. Continue as the track winds left, down through an old farmyard, until it meets a road running parallel to the river.

Turn right to walk on the grass bank beside the river. The path is surfaced but overgown. Climb the stile to the right of the bridge parapet and turn left. Cross the bridge and turn left again to drop down to follow the path beside the river. The buildings of Chartham Paper Mill, visible in the distance, mark our destination. Pass the marvellous lake on your right where you will see examples of the wildfowl normally associated with lakes of this nature. Keep your eyes peeled along the river banks for kingfishers.

Climb up and over an embankment, following a set of steps, and continue along the well defined path. Cross a grassy track, walking as

The Old Bakery at Chartham.

close to the river as you can. Pass another large lake on your right. Shortly after, and before reaching a kissing gate, you will see a rustic picnic table and benches, where you may pause to tarry a while and take in the surrounding countryside. Go through the gate and follow a path which has been surfaced in order to allow the less able bodied a chance to enjoy both the river and surrounding countryside.

When you reach the main road turn left to follow the village street back to the Artichoke.

15 Elham
The King's Arms

Elham is a delightful downland settlement, one of the prettiest villages in Kent. It has at its heart an ancient square surrounded on three sides by timber-frame buildings, and on its fourth by the impressive and imposing church. The main street boasts a picturesque Tudor hotel and a scattering of small shops intermixed with domestic dwellings. The King's Arms is located in the square, directly opposite the church. It started life as a 16th century coaching inn, and has an archway leading to the old beamed lounge bar at the rear of the inn with its unusual open fireplace, barrel tables and exposed beams with authentic cobwebs. There is also a garden at the rear. Children are welcome in both of these locations, though not the public bar.

The menu is extensive and ranges from jacket potatoes and steak and kidney pie to mouth-watering steaks. All main meals are served with fresh seasonal vegetables and half portions are available for children. Vegetarians are also catered for. A traditional roast is on offer on Sundays, for which it is advisable to book. There are Flowers and Fremlins beers and three real ales, including Old Baily. Heineken and Stella Artois are among the lagers. You will also find Scrumpy Jack cider.

The opening hours are 11 am to 3 pm and 6 pm to 11 pm on weekdays and from 12 noon to 3 pm and 6 pm to 11 pm on Sundays. Telephone: 01303 840242.

How to get there: Elham lies between Barham, to the north, and Lyminge, to the south, on a minor road joining the A20 and the A2.

Parking: Parking is available in the village square in front of the King's Arms.

Length of the walk: 3½ miles. Map: OS Pathfinder 1231 (inn GR 177439).

The walk is an exhilarating journey over rolling downland and through woodland and hidden valleys. You may have to huff and perhaps even puff, but any effort will be richly rewarded and the elevated views across the open countryside and down onto the village of Elham itself are breathtaking (in the other sense of the word).

The Walk

From the King's Arms turn left into Cock Lane, bounded on both sides by some charming old properties. At the end of the lane go through a gate and head diagonally right across the field, crossing the stream before reaching and then negotiating another gate. Cross the field as it goes uphill in front of you towards a stile, clearly visible in the fenceline in front of you. You will enjoy a marvellous feeling of spaciousness as you head gently uphill and across to your right you will see the radio masts at Tolsford Hill.

Cross the stile and continue, following the fenceline as it curves around to your left. As the fence bends left stop and look behind you at the sleepy little village of Elham nestled beneath you and the majestic, rolling countryside behind it. The terrain here lends itself to sitting down and letting your eyes 'ramble' over this superb tranche of English countryside, with the Elham valley stretching to your left and right.

Eventually climb another stile and turn to your right. Continue on the track in front of you across an arable field to a fenceline where you turn right. Follow the grassy bank to the road. Turn left and continue along the road, with views across open fields to your right. Although this is a quiet country lane be attentive to road traffic at all times. Turn left at the T-junction and then almost immediately right to walk through the busy farmyard of Standard Hill Farm to the large farm gates. Go through and head down the slope of another marvellous pastoral valley to a stile beside a gate. Continue in the same direction

70

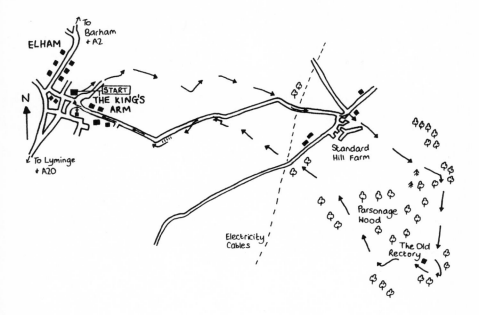

and then follow the easily discernible track as it wends up the other side to run to the left of woodland. Ignore all the stiles on your right and drop in and out of a small hollow. When you have almost reached the far corner of the field turn right through a gate into woodland and then through another gate to cross an arable field.

You will see clearly a gap in the fencing on the far side of the field. Aim to pass through the gate at this point. Keep the fenceline to your right as you proceed through a sparse orchard to a stile next to a telegraph pole in front of the Old Rectory. Turn left and follow the track. At the end of the drive turn immediately right to follow a woodland trackway. (This route has been diverted and may therefore be shown differently on your OS maps.)

At the crossroads of woodland paths carry straight on, dropping downhill in an old sunken lane bounded by chestnut trees – marvellous in the autumn. At the bottom of the slope turn right through a gate and head diagonally right across the valley, aiming for the right-hand edge of the woodland in front of you. Here you pass through another gate and go over the rise, aiming to pass firstly to the left of a solitary tree, the top of which is just visible to you, and then by the right-hand edge of more woodland to go through a gate. Follow the field edge and woodland boundary to your left as you drop down

Standard Hill Farm, near Elham.

into and out of another valley, aiming for the electricity pylon in the distance. The views to your right are idyllic, with sheep and cattle grazing.

Cross the road and follow the bridleway as it passes underneath the high tension cables. Go through yet another gate and continue to follow the field edge path as it first turns right and then left to run almost parallel to the road. The village of Elham starts to unfold beneath you again. Continue downhill, keeping the fence to your right, until you reach a stile which you climb to follow a track down to the road. Turn left to follow this sunken lane as it leads you eventually back uphill to the village square. Digress, if you haven't already done so, to explore one of the loveliest churches in the county.

16 Reculver
The King Ethelbert

Reculver, on the north Kent coastline, is a pleasing mixture of the old and the new. The Romans built a fort here in the 3rd century AD and King Ethelbert, one of the first of our Christian kings, had a church constructed inside the walls in the 6th century. The King Ethelbert pub was originally the vicarage but has been an inn since 1843. The interior retains a marvellous atmosphere, with exposed oak beams in the front bar, and both bars boast an open fire during winter months.

A large range of beers are available, normally Flowers and Fremlins. Real ales are also on offer although these vary, Old Speckled Hen being an example, with Scrumpy Jack and Strongbow on draught for the cider drinkers. Lager enthusiasts are not forgotten, with Heineken, Heineken Export and Stella Artois on draught and bottled Kronenbourg. The menu is extensive, ranging from a cheese sandwich to a T-bone steak. Daily specials include chilli con carne and various curries, all of which are home-made. The meals are complemented with fresh vegetables and there is a traditional roast on Sundays. There is a large garden with an action tree for children to play upon and they are also welcome inside the pub, as indeed are dogs.

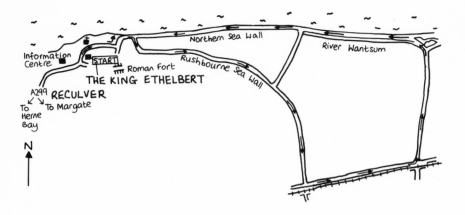

The times of opening are daily from 11 am to 3 pm and 7 pm to 11 pm in the winter months and from 11 am to 11 pm during the summer.

Telephone: 01227 374368.

How to get there: Reculver sits between the larger coastal resorts of Margate and Herne Bay. Follow the signs from the A299 Thanet Way. The pub can be found at the far end of the village, just beneath the twin towers, which provide an excellent aiming point.

Parking: There is ample car parking on the sea front adjacent to the King Ethelbert.

Length of the walk: An easy 3½ miles. Map: OS Pathfinder 1196 (inn GR 226693).

The walk lets you explore the remains of King Ethelbert's church and that part of the Roman fort that has not been lost to the sea. Erosion has been busy along this shoreline. The route then takes you out into the remoteness of the surrounding agricultural land, following the raised sea wall. The return leg provides broad, open views across the North Sea. The seabirds and inland wildfowl are prodigious at all times of the year, and marshland watercourses are a haven for butterflies, dragonflies and other resident insects during the summer months. The walk is easily negotiable, with no stiles or hills to climb.

The Walk

From the pub turn towards the sea, following the tarmac path towards and then past Reculver Towers, the remains of the church built by King Ethelbert. The church was constructed inside the walls of a Roman fort, built here in the 3rd century AD. Erosion by the sea since

Roman times has washed away a large part of the fort. You can either explore the remaining part now or, if you prefer, upon your return.

Turn left onto a broad track leading to the sea. Turn right to follow the sea wall. Pass in front of the water inlet and then turn right, through a field gate, to follow the grassy sea defence wall which leads off in front of you. Continue to follow the wall as it bends to the left and winds its way out into the marshes. The sea is obscured from your view now but these inland marshes are crisscrossed by watercourses bounded by reeds and you may well get a glimpse of the grey herons, swans or other wildfowl that seek cover in these waterways.

In the distance to your right you will see the traffic on the busy Thanet Way. You will probably also notice trains on the railway line, which eventually you reach. Turn left to continue parallel to the line. In front of you now are superb views across the marsh to the Thanet coastal resort of Minnis Bay in the far distance.

Ignore the waymarked crossing point over the railway to your right but continue in the same direction until you reach the next waymarked crossing point. Turn left, away from the railway line, to follow a broad track bounded on either side by arable fields, which leads you to the sea wall in the distance.

Turn left onto the paved sea wall path, with the broad expanse of the North Sea on your right. Gulls and other seabirds either skim the

Reculver Marshes.

surface or seem to glide without pattern or purpose in the skies above.

Simply follow the sea wall towards the twin towers in the distance, and then upon reaching the remains of the church retrace your steps to the King Ethelbert.

Places of interest nearby

The *Reculver Country Park* is a delightful place to stroll and, in the summer, a good place for picnics. The park is a renowned site for bird watchers and is well placed for the twice yearly spectacle of migrating birds, arriving from and departing to, warmer climes. An interpretation centre has displays on the geology, history and wildlife of the area.

17 Stodmarsh
The Red Lion

Stodmarsh is a small and extremely isolated village of intrinsic charm with a scattering of houses, the pub and a marvellous church which simply begs exploration. The Red Lion has stood here since 1452 and parts of the original building still remain visible to the eye. There is a wonderful atmosphere and a welcome for visitors. You will find two open log fires to sit beside in winter months, one in a big brick fireplace. An extremely interesting feature is the floors. No wall to wall carpeting here but floorboards and York stone to walk on.

Beers on offer include Adnams and Greene King IPA and Abbot Ale. Draught Guinness is served and for the lager drinker both draught Kronenbourg and Harp are available. Cider drinkers may like to try Theobalds Kentish or the more traditional Dry Blackthorn. The menu is extensive and the main courses are extremely varied and imaginative. These range from ploughman's lunches to vegetable curry, stir fry, venison, halibut and gravadlaz (salmon and herbs if, like me, you did not know). A traditional roast and set meal is offered on Sunday. There are also a range of home-made puddings – especially favoured is the treacle tart. Children and dogs are welcome and there is a large garden at the rear.

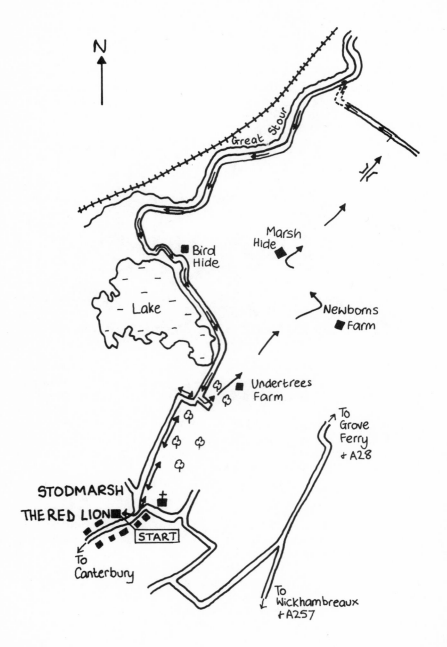

N

Great Stour

Bird Hide

Marsh Hide

Lake

Newborns Farm

Undertrees Farm

To Grove Ferry & A28

STODMARSH

THE RED LION

START

To Canterbury

To Wickhambreaux & A257

The Red Lion is open all day during the week from 11 am to 11 pm. The Sunday hours are 12 noon to 3 pm and 6.30 pm to 10.30 pm. Telephone: 01227 721339.

How to get there: Stodmarsh lies to the north-east of Canterbury between the villages of Upstreet and Wickhambreaux. Approaching from the north, leave the A28 at Upstreet, signposted 'Grove Ferry, Preston, Wickhambreaux' and simply follow this road towards Wickhambreaux. Stodmarsh will be signposted to your right. From the south leave the A257 at Littlebourne and, having gone through the village of Wickhambreaux, simply follow the signs to Stodmarsh.

Parking: There is limited car parking at the Red Lion and in the village street. You will, however, find a large car park at the Stodmarsh Nature Reserve, off the track which leaves the village by the Red Lion.

Length of the walk: 3½ miles. Map: OS Pathfinder 1196 (inn GR 219605).

The walk takes you into the Stodmarsh Nature Reserve, which is the largest area of reed beds in the county. It is easy walking on a flat terrain with abundant interest at any time of the year, although, for many, winter and spring are favourite times to visit. A place for field guides, binoculars and total relaxation.

Dogs, of course, should be kept on leads in the reserve.

The Walk

From the Red Lion turn left on the road towards the church. Almost immediately turn left to follow the track running between whitewashed properties and the petite triangular village green. The track becomes a broad lane, bounded on both sides by mature hedges, as it passes the Nature Conservancy Council car park, with occasional views across open fields to your left. At the end of the lane turn right to follow another broad track, which runs in essence on a causeway. This is bounded on one side by a vast expanse of reed beds which in turn edge the lake around whose most southerly boundary we are now walking, albeit that the density of the reeds is such that the lake itself is not apparent. The lens caps on your binoculars should now be removed and your bird books researched, for the reed beds and this whole area provide shelter for both some of the rarer as well as the more common of our bird life. There is cover for reed buntings, sedge and reed warblers, Savi's warbler and bearded reedling, with ospreys and hen and marsh harriers visiting the reserve on migration.

Eventually the pathway meets a staggered junction of paths. Ignore the first track going off to your right but take the second (signposted

The Great Stour at Stodmarsh.

'Marsh Hide'), ignoring as you pass them two footbridges crossing the watercourses to your left and right. At the end of the track turn left to follow a broad track, keeping the watercourse to your right, with views across open fields. As you get closer to the farm buildings, cross the footbridge (you are warned at this point that occasionally grazing stock are in the field and that all dogs should be kept on a lead) and turn left, following a defined path towards two more footbridges clearly evident in the distance, both of which you cross. Turn left towards the bird hide in front of you. Do enter the hide to view the considerable number of wildfowl that in winter months reside on the reserve, mallard and teal, wigeon and wild geese.

Turn right in front of the hide to follow a broad track with a raised clay bund to your left and open reed beds to your right. Go through a kissing gate and then diagonally right to climb a stile beside a gate and follow another broad track. Eventually pass a footbridge on your right and cross over the bridge in front of you to enter a pasture field, keeping in a straight line to meet the right-hand edge of the field. Follow the reed-bounded field edge until you meet a broad track. Turn left and follow this well defined track until you reach the river wall, where you turn left to walk beside the Great Stour on a defined pathway.

Eventually the path turns inland again from the river and, at this point, you are following the Lampen Wall, built as a flood defence barrier in the 18th century by Flemish engineers. Soon Stodmarsh Lake becomes visible and the path now follows its eastern shore. Diving ducks like pochard and tufted duck and the resident group of cormorants are nearly almost always in residence. Pass the bird hide, which gives elevated views across the lake, and follow the well defined path which leads you easily back to the point at which you deviated earlier, and then you simply retrace your steps back to the village of Stodmarsh and the Red Lion.

18 Staple
The Black Pig

Staple is a village that, because of its location to the south of the main Canterbury to Sandwich road, is often overlooked. It was much busier in the 19th century, however, when local and neighbouring landowners attended its market where fleeces were sold. In fact the name Staple means 'wool market'. The parish covers a large area but has relatively few inhabitants. The black-beamed Tudor façade of the Black Pig is so impressive. It simply oozes history and so it should, dating, as it does, back to the time when King Henry VIII was ruling this land. The pub functioned as a brewery until 1926 and up until 1949 it also undertook the role of village shop and newsagent's. The brewery vault still exists but has been sealed.

You are really spoilt for choice here with an extensive food menu available in all bars. Traditional pub fare ranges from sandwiches to half pound burgers or even a black pudding butty. The menu board offers a further selection, which includes minted lamb chops, steak and kidney pie, meat or vegetable lasagne, scampi, breaded plaice or steaks, from a 6-8 oz fillet to a 20 oz rump. All meals are served with either fresh vegetables or chips and a salad. To extend the choice even more the daily specials board lists other dishes. Desserts include meringue surprise, treacle tart or chocolate fudge cake. The children's menu offers all their favourites. With a large secluded garden and children welcome in both the restaurant and the two bars the Black Pig is ideal for families. The public bar retains the typical tradition of an English pub with its dartboard and pool table. John Smith's and Master Brew are on draught and there are normally a good selection of real ales from the handpump. These change regularly but you may find Wadworth 6X or Tolly Original. Draught Scrumpy Jack and bottled Woodpecker ciders are also available, as indeed are Beck's, Kronenbourg and Foster's lagers.

The opening hours are from 11 am to 4 pm and 7 pm to 11 pm during the week and from 12 noon to 3 pm and 7 pm to 10.30 pm on Sundays. Food is served from 12 to 2.30 pm and 7 pm to 9.30 pm.

Telephone: 01304 812361.

How to get there: Follow the main Canterbury to Sandwich road, the A257. If approaching from Canterbury turn right shortly after entering the village of Wingham and then follow the signs to Staple. If approaching from Sandwich turn left at Ash and follow the signs. The Black Pig is signposted off Fleming Road.

Parking: You may leave your car in the ample car parking area of the Black Pig.

Length of the walk: 4 miles. Map: OS Pathfinder 1212 (inn GR 278564).

The village is surrounded by a pastoral countryside and, for that reason, although this is one of the longer of the walks in this book it is in no way demanding. The route enables a gentle exploration of the area's diverse agricultural activities, from sheep and orchards to cauliflowers, giving too an opportunity to visit one of the vineyards and perhaps the chance to taste some local English wine.

The Walk

Turn left onto the lane outside the Black Pig and continue, passing as you do the attractive brown and cream, thatched cottage on your right. Shortly after, turn right onto a broad track in front of a white-painted house. Pass the charming, more traditional, thatched cottage on your left. Follow the boundary fence and when this turns away from you, continue across the field in front of you, aiming towards a clearly visible fingerpost in the distance. On your left you will have superb views across open flat countryside and no doubt the church steeple in the distant village of Ash will be a focus of your attention.

Having crossed the field, negotiate a set of rural steps and turn left on top of the bank. Cross the next field, aiming for the black barn just

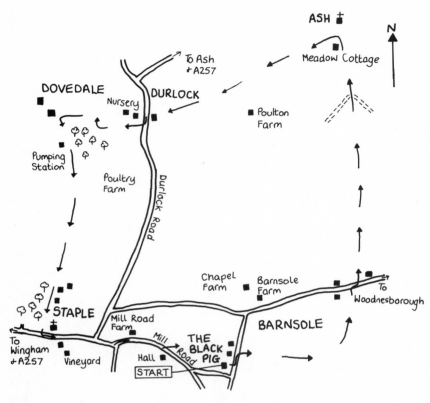

to the right of centre in front of you. Typical Kentish country scenery to your left now with oast houses and synonymous white cowls. Having reached a hedgeline, continue in the same direction, following a grassy track towards buildings in the near distance. Cross the road and follow the broad track that heads towards Ash church, bounded by intensive agricultural fields, normally of cauliflowers or other members of the brassica family.

As the track curves left continue straight on, aiming to the left of the church. On the south facing slope to the right of the church you will see a vineyard. Upon meeting another main track turn left, then follow the grassy bank to the left-hand side of the ditch.

Follow the ditch as it heads towards a hedgerow. Turn right to follow the headland beside the hedge and at the point where the hedge is replaced by a fence climb a stile on your left. Go through a gate and cross a broad track to another gate, beside a marvellous old willow tree. Cross the open field to the right of the telegraph pole, following a well defined path. The track broadens out and crosses a small culvert to follow the right-hand edge of a small stream. The track then takes you diagonally right into the corner of the field through a gap to then continue beside a very mature hedgeline.

The farm buildings of Poulton Farm will be visible to your left as indeed will be a line of trees that seem to descend in order of superiority from grandfather at the front to junior who appears to be bringing up the rear.

Cross a stile. Turn right for 20 yards and then turn left to follow the right-hand side of a ditch across arable land. Vast open stretches of open agricultural land seem to stretch as far as the eye can see off to your left. Focusing the eye, however, is the little hamlet of Durlock.

Turn left at the road and after 20 yards turn right to follow a track through trees to enter a fruit orchard. Turn right and follow a broad track around the edge of the orchard, eventually passing a hop garden, until you reach a working farmyard. Turn left behind a barn to follow another broad track gently downhill. Pass the pumping station and continue, to cross a stile into a huge arable field. The path runs to the right of the telegraph poles (one has a broad yellow blaze to assist you) that you can easily discern in front of you. Use these as your aiming point and proceed across the field towards Staple church in the far distance.

A thatched cottage at Staple.

Go through the gap in the hedge in the field boundary and continue in the same direction to the road. Turn left and follow the road, passing Staple Vineyard at Church Farm.

Continue on the road and as it bends left follow the road in front of you (signposted 'Chillenden' and 'Aylesham'), known as Buckland Lane. Just before you reach the village hall take the second of two public rights of way that go off to your left. Head across the field to a line of poplar trees, aiming to the right of the barn. The path initially takes you to the right of this barn. After 150 yards the path bends left towards the poplar trees. Here you go through a gap to follow a defined track to the road, where you turn right to return to the Black Pig.

Places of interest nearby
St James' church is notable for a Saxon window and an unusual one-handed clock on the west side of the tower, donated by Lady Groves in 1789 on condition she be able to see it from her home. Passed late on the walk is *Staple Vineyard* and you will be welcomed here for self-guided tours from Easter to September. The vineyard shop is open 10 am to 5 pm (12 noon to 4 pm on Sundays). Telephone 01304 812571.

⑲ Kingsdown
The Zetland Arms

Kingsdown is an elegant village from which the famous White Cliffs seem to emerge. It has a wonderful linear centre, known as The Street, which straggles downhill, bordered on both sides by marvellous properties both old and new, and which begs to be explored. The Zetland Arms is right by the sea and you can sit in the front bar or on the terrace outside and watch the shipping plying the English Channel. Inside, as you would expect, there is a nautical air and charts showing the position of buoys, wrecks and sandbars. The open fire may not be authentic yet it nonetheless provides welcome warmth on bracing days.

This pub is very popular at weekends and, as well as soaking up the views from the beach, customers may enjoy a number of different beers including Ruddles, Shepherd Neame Master Brew and Webster's. For the lager drinker there is also a choice, which normally includes Heineken, Carlsberg and Foster's. Cider drinkers are not forgotten, with Strongbow Dry and Woodpecker Sweet to slake their thirst. The menu board displays a range of freshly cooked meals. These may include fishuns, which is a Chinese dish with spices, BBQ chicken breast and excellent steaks, all served with fresh vegetables.

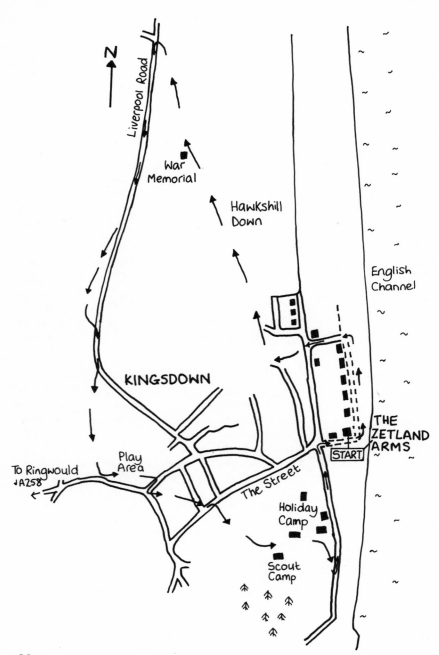

If you still have room then desserts such as pecan nut pie and cream or Cumber fudge cake might tempt you. Children are welcome although there is no special children's menu.

The Zetland Arms is open on Monday to Saturday from 11 am to 2.30 pm and 6 pm to 11 pm. On Sunday the hours are 12 noon to 3 pm and 7 pm to 10.30 pm.

Telephone: 01304 364888.

How to get there: From the road between Dover and Deal, the A258, follow the signposts to Kingsdown. Wind across country, down the picturesque village street and at the crossroads go straight across on a shingle track towards the sea. The Zetland Arms is on your left.

Parking: There is reasonable car parking on the compacted shingle in front of the Zetland Arms. Otherwise you can park in The Street in the village of Kingsdown itself.

Length of the walk: 3 miles. Map: OS Pathfinder 1232 (inn GR 380485).

The first part of the walk takes us gently uphill to give elevated views across the English Channel, and then turns inland amidst some marvellous rolling countryside. The second half brings us back into Kingsdown itself with a chance to explore the village further and finally the opportunity to top up our ozone levels as we negotiate the final leg beside the sea itself.

The Walk

On leaving the Zetland Arms turn left and follow the broad, shingle track between residential dwellings to your left and the scattered maritime dross and beach huts to your right. Follow the narrow, surfaced path, its entrance marked by white posts, put up no doubt to discourage motor vehicles, until you reach the boundary road where you turn left. Cross the road in front of you and pass through the rusty iron railings to follow the footpath as it gently ascends the slope ahead.

When you reach the crossroads of public paths turn right and when this path divides take the right-hand fork to follow a well defined path, with a hedge to your left and close-boarded fencing to your right. Cross a broad track to follow the path as it heads across fields. Here the views open up and from this elevated position marvellous views of the English Channel and the ships plying their business can be obtained. Follow the path as it wends gently uphill. At the top of this rise the path then continues straight and true towards the church. To the right of the church in the far distance you can also see the rounded chimneys of the Reculver power station.

The Street, Kingsdown.

This area through which we are walking was used as an aerodrome during the First World War and you see evidence of this as you pass the war memorial dedicated to the gallant airmen who gave their lives in France and were stationed at Walmer Aerodrome from April 1917 to October 1918.

Ignoring the track to your left, continue on the path as it runs parallel to the sea. Ahead you will notice two strategically placed benches. Just after the second, take the mown track as it goes off left, heading for a point between the white-boarded weather vane and the church. Follow this as it leads gently downhill to a private road where you turn right to reach the main road (at this point known as Liverpool Road) where you turn left. Continue along the road. As you will note it changes its name and becomes Glen Road for no obvious or apparent reason. Shortly after, ignore the footpath signposted to your right, but almost immediately take the signposted bridleway which goes off to the right and runs almost parallel to the road. Follow this delightful old track, bounded on both sides by trees and hedge. An obvious autumnal delight.

When you reach a crossroads of woodland paths, turn left to follow a path going slightly uphill and curving around to meet the road. Turn right and follow the road uphill, with outstanding views across open farmland on your right to the disused windmill at Ringwould visible, although framed by trees, in the distance. When the road curves to the left take the public bridleway signstoned on your right and follow a broad track across agricultural land, using the tree-topped mound in the far distance as your aiming point.

Two adult paces from the road turn left and aim to walk with the fence to the play area on your left. If you have young children with you take advantage of the strategically placed picnic table to sit and contemplate the views across the English Channel, whilst your children work off excess energy on the cleverly designed play equipment. Continue on the narrow path and, after having passed through the second of two staggered barriers, take the path that goes off immediately to your right to the road, where you turn right and head uphill.

At the road junction take the footpath signposted to your left and follow a narrow path between hedges and close-boarded fences downhill, continuing on a footway to reach Alexandra Road where you turn right to another road, The Street. Turn left and head downhill for 25 yards before turning right onto a footpath between residential properties, which leads gradually uphill into a small copse of trees. Take care as this path could be very slippery at certain times. At the T-junction take the left-hand fork. When you reach the mown area bear to your right and then turn left to go downhill on a broad path running beside the boundary fence of the International Scout Camp until you negotiate a set of steps to the road beside the sea. Turn left and either follow this road to South Road, where you turn right to get back to the Zetland Arms, or if you still have the energy digress across the shingle beach to follow the line of the tide back to the pub, which is clearly visible in the distance. It's hard on the legs, mind!

⓴ St Margaret's at Cliffe
The Cliffe Tavern

The village of St Margaret's at Cliffe sits at the top and St Margaret's Bay nestles at the base of the famous White Cliffs with their toes in the English Channel. This splendid white weatherboarded public house sits in the heart of the village. It is a building that dates back to the 16th century and was, at one time, a school house. The bars are extremely welcoming and the Cliffe Tavern has a marvellous ambience, enhanced by two open fireplaces.

The menu ranges from traditional bar meals, such as fish and chips, to pheasant casseroles, scallop and salmon in puff pastry with a lemon sauce and grilled T-bone steaks, although some of the more adventurous dishes may only be available in the evenings so it may be best to check. Desserts include home-made lemon meringue, deluxe trifles or fresh citrus fruit salad and cream. Vegetable pastas are also available and on Sundays a traditional lunch is served. Children are welcome, although there is no specific child's menu. A good meal needs a good accompaniment and beer drinkers can choose from an extensive selection including Wadworth 6X, Abbot Ale and Shepherd Neame Master Brew and Bishops Finger. Lager drinkers have draught Kronenbourg, Beck's and the Czechoslovakian Budvar. Cider drinkers may like to try the draught Olde English.

The Cliffe Tavern is open from 11 am to 3 pm and 6 pm to 11.30 pm on Monday to Saturday, and on Sunday from 12 noon to 3.30 pm and 7 pm to 10.30 pm.
Telephone: 01304 852400.

How to get there: Leave the road between Dover and Deal, the A258, signposted 'St Margaret's'. Once in the village you will find the Cliffe Tavern on your left opposite the church.

Parking: There is a spacious car park at the rear of the pub, and additional parking in the nearby public car park.

Length of the walk: 3 miles. Map: OS Pathfinder 1232 (inn GR 359448).

The first half of the walk explores the village and becomes a little more strenuous as it takes you up to the cliff top. It soon becomes easier as you pass the old disused windmill to reach the South Foreland lighthouse. The return leg is through open countryside, followed by a chance to see more of the village of St Margaret's itself. This is a great area for binoculars — not only for shipping but also to appreciate the many migrant birds during spring and autumn.

St Margaret's Bay.

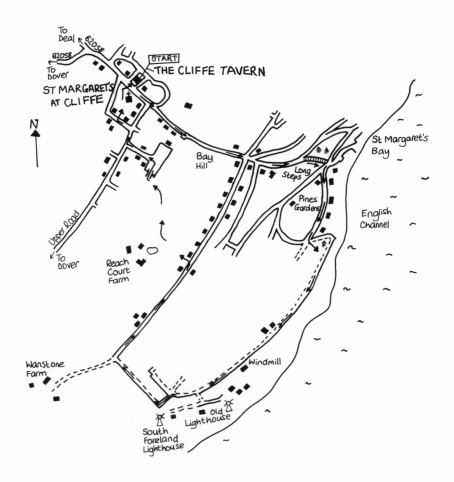

The Walk

Leave the Cliffe Tavern and go back into the High Street. Turn left, crossing the road to follow the footway. Continue on the footway as it proceeds down through the village street. At one point it ceases but keep on the right-hand side of the road until you are able to rejoin the footway again. Continue to follow the footway as it drops down into a little valley, with wonderful views across open fields on your left to the sea in the distance.

Climb the other side and when you reach St Margaret's Road running off to your right you will see a marvellous vista of open sea in front of you. Carry on in the same direction, following a raised

94

embankment on the top of which is a narrow path. Continue to follow this. Rejoin the footway before embarking down a steep flight of steps known as 'the Long Steps'. Please be very careful as you negotiate these as they can be somewhat uneven and extremely slippery in wet conditions.

At the bottom of the steps turn right onto a private road, signposted 'Pines Garden and Museum'. Turning almost immediately left again, continue along Beach Road, with gracious residential properties to your left and the splendidly landscaped Pines Garden to your right, until you reach a crossroads of tracks at the extreme boundary of the gardens.

Turn left and take the broad track as it winds gradually uphill to the cliff top. Turn right and follow a broad, grassy track, admiring as you do the elevated views of the English Channel beneath you – and, on a clear day, the French coastline in the distance. During spring and summer months the cliff tops are bedecked with chalk maritime plants and flowers which in turn attract a wide variety of butterflies.

Eventually the track becomes metalled as it heads towards and to the right of the windmill in the distance. Continuing in the same direction, you now see the South Foreland lighthouse, our next focal point.

As the path gently descends turn left to follow the broad road leading to the lighthouse. At the T-junction with a narrower track turn to your left, heading towards the sea, to obtain better views of the old lighthouse that guided sailors through one of the world's busiest sea lanes since its construction in 1843. It was one of the first lighthouses to be worked by electricity and the radio pioneer Marconi carried out a number of experiments here. It is no longer in use today but it is open to the public at weekends and on bank holiday Mondays from April to the end of October. If the lighthouse is closed make the most of it from the outside before commencing the return leg of the walk. Retrace your steps to follow again the path past the entrance, and then continue across the broad entrance road negotiated earlier to take a narrow, surfaced path with woodland to your right and open fields to the left. At the T-junction ignore the footpath going off across fields in front of you and turn right to follow another broad track.

Continue until you reach, on your right, the property known as Southolme. Turn left to follow a narrow track, passing a bungalow on your right-hand side and woodland to your left. Continue across the stile and then follow the well marked track that goes diagonally to your right-hand side towards the housing estate that you can see in the distance.

You are now walking across an open field, with the Reach Court farmhouse to your left. Climb the stile and follow a surfaced track between hedgerows defining the back gardens of adjoining properties. Turn right when you meet the road and cross to the other footway. Follow this footway as it wends off to your left and then right and then left again around the very neat housing development.

When you come out of Reach Close next to a red telephone box turn right. After approximately 30 yards turn left to follow a narrow, partially-surfaced track. Take the next wide track on your right, which runs down between residential houses, passing a white and black fronted house on your right-hand side. Continue on this grassy track as it leads you to the rear of the church, and then you simply follow the path as it winds through the churchyard and returns you to the Cliffe Tavern.

Places of interest nearby
The *South Foreland lighthouse* opens 2 pm to 5.30 pm at weekends (and on bank holiday Mondays) from April to October. Telephone 01892 890651 for further details.